Get It Across Loud and Clear

Get It Across Loud and Clear

A speaker's practical guide to preparation and delivery

Ali Martin

Authentic

First published 2012 by Authentic Media Limited
52 Presley Way, Crownhill, Milton Keynes, MK8 0ES
www.authenticmedia.co.uk

British Library Cataloguing in Publication Data

A catalogue record for this book is available from the British Library

ISBN 978-1-85078-993-2

Cover design by Peter Barnsley
Printed and Bound in Great Britain by CPI Group (UK), Ltd, Croydon, CR0 4YY

**This book is dedicated to three brilliant men:
Dad, Mike and Joel**

Dad – for your unconditional love, for always being proud of me, for modelling from the word go what it is to love Jesus wholeheartedly and to point others to him.

Mike – for believing in me, cheering me on, giving me room to both fail and grow. I have learned so much from you.

Joel – you are God's gift to me; all I want and need.

Acknowledgments

It's taken me so long to write this book and there are many people to thank for their help along the way. So (deep breath!) thank you to . . .

My contributors. What a privilege it was to pick your brains and learn from you. This book is so much the stronger for your wisdom and input.

Dad and Andy for going through the manuscript in incredible detail and with amazing patience – your suggestions and additions were so helpful.

My mum for spending extra hours with the gorgeous William so I could finish the book. I am so thankful for you, Mum and Nana.

Liza, for reading my early attempts, but more importantly being the best encourager and friend a girl could have.

Mike for many things – not least of all for writing the foreword (and getting it done on time!).

My NCT mums, especially Beth, who persistently encouraged me until the book was finished.

The team at Authentic, especially Mark Finnie for his willingness to publish this book in the first place.

The wonderfully patient, kind and gentle Jess Bee, my editor.

The staff and family of Soul Survivor Watford, who have graciously allowed me to practise both my speaking and my feedback-giving on them.

Jez, Lynzi, Joel, Noah, Jake and Ben – I started writing this book in your beautiful home in Solvang. Joel and I loved that month when we got to be part of your family.

My friends and family, especially Joel, William and Esther. I am blessed, beyond what I deserve, to have you all in my life.

Contents

Foreword

This book is an utter gem. It cannot be anything but helpful to anyone who wants to develop their communication skills. It is practical, insightful, biblical, funny, engaging and brilliant. A book on communication needs to communicate well and this does it magnificently. It is clear and accessible, as well as full of truth and wisdom. Whether you are just setting out and think you are called to preach or teach, or have been doing this for years, this book will help you progress to the next level.

One of the great needs in today's church is for preaching that effectively communicates. Most theological colleges rightly focus on teaching theology, but there is little emphasis on how best to impart biblical knowledge to others. The truth of God's Word deserves to be communicated in the most effective way and, as Ali says in her introduction, most teachers have something good to say, they just don't always know how to say it. Of course we must have a message, and one of the strengths of this book is that Ali focuses on the art of preparing talks, which are biblically grounded, in order to see lives transformed.

Ali has been my friend and close colleague for more years than we would both like to admit. She is as she comes across in this book: warm, friendly, fun, honest, vulnerable, insightful, and she's also a great team player. She is the real thing. She is also one of the best Bible teachers I know (despite what she says!). Her interviews with friends who are also passionate about communicating the gospel are helpful, illuminating and add an extra layer of depth to an already brilliant book.

This is the best book on communication I have ever read, written by one of the best people I have ever met. I wholeheartedly commend it to you.

Mike Pilavachi
Soul Survivor

Introduction – Setting the Scene

Why write a book about speaking and why buy a book about speaking? Because I want you to be the best speaker you can possibly be, and everyone gets better with input.

A few years ago I went to a seminar. I was desperate to hear what the speaker had to say: the topic was one I was interested in, and being clueless on the subject I was both hungry for information and ready to take on board what I heard. Armed with my notebook and pen, I really did try my best, I promise, to concentrate and be attentive. The trouble was I just couldn't decipher the message through the dull and confused hour-long waffle. I do realize this sounds harsh, but you weren't there and though generally I try to be quite nice, I just want to be honest with you. Anyway, I left disappointed and frustrated at not receiving the teaching I'd been so looking forward to and at having wasted an hour of a precious Saturday morning. I'm still not sure what the speaker was getting at, and I'm still none the wiser on the subject covered.

The purpose of my honest/harsh (delete as appropriate) reflections is to get to the point of sharing this: in my experience, I've found that most speakers have good things to say. They are generally diligent in waiting on God, in study and in preparation. I am (fairly) convinced that the speaker on the

aforementioned wasted Saturday morning did have something of worth to communicate. There was almost certainly a
message inside that really did want to get out. But in that
case, and all too often in others, there's a huge gap between
what's bubbling within and what actually comes forth.

And that's why I'm writing this book. My aim is to encourage you to develop your speaking gift. Not just so that you
would be better, good or even excellent, but in order that you
will be more effective in communicating God's truth and
heart. The ultimate aim is that people would hear and understand, grow closer to God, and become more like Jesus – rely-
ing less on themselves and more on God. The hope is that as
we work together at honing our communication skills we will
be a blessing to those who give us their attention. We don't
want to leave people wanting to poke their own eyes out to
stay awake, like me on that fateful Saturday. Whether someone is listening out of delight (our mums) or duty (the poor
person who fully intended to fake a coughing fit at the end of
the worship but got stuck in the middle of a row with no obvious escape route), we want to bring something of worth that
would not only engage but equip them in life, and draw them
into a deeper relationship with God and a love of his Word.

You are probably reading this book because you are either in
a situation where you currently preach or teach, or feel that this
is something you would like to do. So it's probably important to
clarify what we mean by 'preaching' and 'teaching'. Both words
are commonly used in the Bible and often go hand in hand (see
1 Tim. 4:13, for example). Simply put, preaching is about proclaiming and announcing, whereas teaching is about instructing
and explaining. This is why we regularly see the two terms
together – preaching proclaims what God has done, teaching
unpacks the implications. In this book, I use the terms inter-
changeably (along with the term 'speak') as most messages
given in church have elements of both, even if certain types of
messages or speakers lean more towards one than the other.

I am assuming you want to learn about speaking in a church context, that you are someone who gets up in front of a group and tries to open up the Bible to others in some way. Having said that, the principles can often be carried forward into a wider sphere, and my hope and prayer is that it will also equip and encourage you in all different types of communication.

Whatever you're doing, I love that you're reading this book. It says that you are committed to developing the gift God has given you; not content to stay as you are, and not wishfully thinking that God will miraculously download a stunning bit of brain software to turn you into a world-class communicator overnight. A friend of mine once said of songwriting, that it's '10 per cent inspiration and 90 per cent perspiration' (I've not credited him as I'm fairly sure he stole the line from someone else, like most of us do). The same can be said of communicating. The fact that you're reading this says that you're committed to getting sweaty, and that makes me happy. The people who listen to you really do deserve that much and I reckon they'll thank you for it.

I'm not writing this book because I think I've got all the answers. It isn't that I've mastered the art of teaching and preaching, or that I've successfully fanned my gift into flame and now want to fan yours too. It's really not that at all. I have had to get past all kinds of doubts and insecurities in order to put fingertips to keypad and write this book. I am so far from being an expert, a million miles off from having this subject all sewn up. I'm constantly kicking myself, learning, trying to get better, putting into practice the feedback I receive, and wanting to be able to look back and see that I've progressed in my preaching. Sometimes I'm encouraged. More often I'm frustrated.

But somewhere along the way God has put a passion in my heart to do this journey with others, and after spending some years helping people in my local church in their communication, I have come to see something simple: everyone gets better with input, and with someone to point out the blindingly obvious, as well as the not so apparent. Although I'm not sitting in front of you, taking notes and making observations, that's what I'm trying to do through this book – to give you a little bit of input, attempt to bring to light any blind spots, and to remind you of the main and the plain – the things that should be so obvious, but are easily forgotten.

As you read on you will encounter my thoughts and observations – or at least those I've stolen from others (mainly my friends, who hopefully won't hold it against me) – as well as bits and pieces I've learned along the way through speaking and hearing others speak. In the pages that follow there are lots of 'top tips' (me throwing out ideas and examples) and sometimes I will be getting quite instructional with you. Please don't think I'm saying that my thoughts and ideas are *the* way, but instead they are a way. I really hope what you read doesn't become a straight-jacket, but instead you're able to receive it as a set of guidelines and pointers to help you as you find your feet or change old habits. Over time you'll find your own rhythm – you'll adopt some of my suggestions and they'll become standard practice, things you'll end up doing naturally and unconsciously. Others will be like a crutch that can be dropped when you find your own style. And still others may be things that you decide you can instantly ditch and forget. In any case, I hope this book helps you grow in the gift God has given you, and that you grow in confidence and ability to serve the people God puts in front of you.

Achieving Greatness

I want you to be the best speaker you can possibly be. If you've never given a talk before, I want to help you start strong. If you have been giving talks for a while, I want to help you to evaluate how you've been doing and to find ways you can improve. William Shakespeare wrote: 'Some are born great, some achieve greatness'.[1] Some speakers are born natural communicators, some are born awful, but everyone can 'achieve greatness'. We can all learn, grow and get better. Everyone can improve.

A Note to the Women

In this book I haven't covered the issue of whether or not it is biblically acceptable for a woman to teach. That's because it's not that kind of book – this is a 'how to' rather than a 'can we?' or 'should we?' kind of book. However, if you're reading this, are female, and in some way feel called to teach and preach, I strongly recommend you spend some time coming to terms with your theology on the subject. Don't avoid it or pretend it's not an issue. Don't be content to find peace in the fact that the men around you seem to think it's OK. Read up on the subject, look at the controversial passages in the Bible, and do your homework, so that you feel comfortable with where you stand on the issue. I've had people offended by me standing up to preach. I've had people who've liked what I've said, but disliked the fact that it has come out of the mouth of a woman. Although it's not pleasant to hear, it doesn't shake me when this happens because I feel comfortable and confident that this is a calling on my life and something the Bible supports. Sooner or later, if you embark on public ministry your authority to speak will be questioned, so it's important that when that day comes you have a firm foundation to stand on.

How to Make this Book Work for You

Before you get started it might help you to know how this book works. We're going to begin with a bit of a foundation, looking at why we speak and what the aims should be as we prepare and deliver talks. These early chapters are grounding us and so are quite theoretical, but when we've covered these basics we will go on to look at more practical things:

* The general preparation of reading the Bible and prayer, followed by the specific preparation of how to begin working on a talk.
* Developing the content and structure of a talk.
* Building in the elements that are going to bring life to your talk – ways to help you connect with and reach your audience,[2] including your delivery of that talk.
* Then as we get towards the end of the book we'll look at how to prepare yourself before giving a talk, and how to review it once it's all done.

Developing a Talk

At the end of the book, there are a couple of pages for your notes that correspond with the content of this book (Appendix 1). The idea is that you make notes on a talk idea as you read, so that by the end of the book you should have a talk in the making, ready for refining.

With a Little Help from My Friends

Some of my friends are amazing communicators (some of the best out there, in my opinion) and I have learned a lot from them over the years, so I asked a few of them if they would share their thoughts on speaking with me. They agreed, and had some great stuff to say. So sprinkled throughout my chapters are the interviews I did with them. I really hope you enjoy them and find them useful.

Pause

As you read this book, you will notice that there are regular opportunities to Pause. You can do this on your own or, even better, with others. When you see a Pause, take time out to reflect, pray and put into practice what you read. This isn't meant to be a book of theory, but instead a collection of ideas to try on for size. If you like them (bearing in mind that all new things feel a little scratchy to begin with), then keep them. If not, then chuck them out or stick them on eBay, metaphorically speaking.

> ### Unpacking a Talk Together
>
> Before you start reading the rest of this book, can I invite you to take a brief detour to the back? Appendix 2 is one of my talks exactly as I prepared it, not quite a transcript, but near enough. As we go through the book, you will, from time to time, see little boxes, just like this one, and each box will unpack what I've been saying in the light of this talk, grounding the theory in practice.

So with all the preamble over, let's get going.

1.

Why Bother? – The Purpose of Preaching and Developing Our Gift

We preach because God calls us to. We work on our preaching because we want to be the most effective we can possibly be for him and his kingdom.

Charles Spurgeon[3] once said: 'If God calls you to be a preacher, do not stoop to be a king.' If we are called to communicate God's truths, I believe we need to value and embrace this calling, and to work hard, putting time and effort in to training so that each of us can be the best communicators we can possibly be. We are going to be looking more at why that is the case later in this chapter. But before we go any further, even though we've only just started, let's pause:

Pause:

Why are you passionate about speaking? What are you hoping to achieve in your preaching?

Here are some of my reflections on why we put ourselves through the hard graft of preparation and the sometimes terrifying ordeal of standing up to preach in the first place.

To Reveal God

When we preach, our aim is to reveal God: his love, grace, mercy, wisdom, kindness, discipline, as well as his plans. We do this by unpacking God's Word. It is in the Bible that we discover God's story, and his character, mission and passion. As we speak we want to bring revelation of who God is to the people that are listening. This is not to add to their knowledge; this is to bring them to the place where their dependence on Father, Son and Holy Spirit is increased; where they say with John the Baptist, 'He must become greater, I must become less' (John 3.30), or as Spurgeon once said, 'I have a great need for Christ; I have a great Christ for my need.'

Every need we have is met in God, and whatever we speak on, and whoever we address, we want to bring a revelation of God.

The Power of the Word

The Bible, the Word of God, is powerful, and therefore the preaching of the Word can change lives. In 2 Timothy 3:16 we are reminded that all Scripture is God-breathed and useful. We want to see lives changed to reflect who God is and how he wants us to live. To help us do that he has given us the model of Jesus, the equipping of the Spirit and his Word. In Hebrews it says: 'For the word of God is living and active. Sharper than any double-edged sword, it penetrates even to dividing soul and spirit, joints and marrow; it judges the thoughts and attitudes of the heart (Heb. 4:12). The Word of God has power to cut away the flesh and 'circumcise the heart' – that is, to change lives, to shave away sinful thoughts, words and deeds, to cut away our selfishness and self-centredness, so that more of Jesus can be revealed. That's the power of the Word of God. To shape and hone and change who we are. When we are called to bring a message from God's Word we need to recognize that his Word is full of power.

The Power of Words

God's Word has power, but I also believe that God has given words in general, power – for good and for bad.

Pause:

Can you think of places in the Bible where we see words of power in action, both positively and negatively? A couple of examples to get you started:

- *In creation God spoke and the universe was formed.*
- *In the Garden of Eden the serpent used persuasive words to tempt and draw Eve.*
- *There are several warnings in the books of Proverbs and James about the effect of words.*

Look also at these specific examples:

'I tell you the truth, whoever hears my word and believes him who sent me has eternal life and will not be condemned; he has crossed over from death to life' (John 5:24).

'Simon Peter answered him, "Lord, to whom shall we go? You have the words of eternal life."' (John 6:68).

God chose to make words powerful. Think of what a word of praise or encouragement can do for us, how that makes us feel. But also, conversely, the damage that can be done by critical, hurtful or negative words. Words are powerful and it's our job to wield that power well – not only when we're preaching but in all of life. When we are called upon to communicate something of God's Word we should be challenged and encouraged that there is a power in what we say, and we should seek God's help in doing that well.

Day in, day out people hear rubbish. Everyone, everyday is bombarded with lies and half-truths. Only Jesus has the words of eternal life. As communicators we have the privilege of bringing words of power, truth and life to people who desperately need to hear them. Because of the power of the Word, and the power of words, preaching is hugely important.

The Bible tells us that some will be called to teach, and assumes that preaching and teaching will be part of spreading the gospel, as well as part of family life together as Christians. Here are a few examples: Jesus commissioned his first followers to go into the world and *preach* the good news (Mark 16:15–16); we read in Romans that those who call on the name of the Lord will be saved, but they can't call on someone they don't believe in, they can't believe in one of whom they've not heard, and they can't hear unless someone *preaches* to them (Rom. 10:13-15). In 1 Timothy, Paul urges Timothy to devote himself to *preaching* and *teaching* and not to neglect his gift:

> Don't let anyone look down on you because you are young, but set an example for the believers in speech, in life, in love, in faith and in purity. Until I come, devote yourself to the public reading of Scripture, to preaching and to teaching. Do not neglect your gift, which was given you through a prophetic message when the body of elders laid their hands on you.
>
> 1 Tim. 4:12–14

Paul continues in 2 Timothy: 'Preach the Word; be prepared in season and out of season; correct, rebuke and encourage – with great patience and careful instruction' (2 Tim. 4:2). We read in both Romans and Ephesians that some are gifted and set apart to *teach* in order to build up the body of Christ (Rom. 12:6-8 and Eph. 4:11–12).

From these examples, it's safe for us to assume that the preaching and teaching of God's Word is not just something for past generations. It's not, in and of itself, old-fashioned and past its sell-by date. That doesn't mean to say that the style of preaching hasn't changed, or that we don't need to find new ways to communicate to a generation maxed out on billion-dollar budget movies. Perhaps people now expect more from a speaker; after all, if something doesn't grab their attention they can usually find something better with the flick of a remote control. We need to communicate in a way that gets and keeps people's interest (and I hope later chapters will be helpful in this), but communicate we must. The truth still has the power to set people free. Good teaching brings revelation of Jesus, it encourages people in their relationship with God and with others, and it reminds them of the truth. The Holy Spirit inspires the preparation and the giving of a talk to cause people to be healed, encouraged, set free, and to go deeper in their understanding of him. Hearing God's Word unpacked and explained challenges others to read the Bible for them-selves and to want to hang out with God more. President Bill Clinton once talked about how the impact of a great speech should not be measured on how beautiful the words are or what people might feel in the moment, but on whether or not the speaker is able to change the way people think and feel. How much more important is this when preaching God's Word? Good preaching should not only cause people to think and feel differently, but live differently as a result of what they hear.

Pause:

Often talks are like good meals – they sustain us, nourish us, keep us healthy, but we can't always remember what we ate several months ago. Having said that, I can remember hearing Mike Pilavachi talk several years ago on finishing the race well. The next day I went for a long walk with a great friend and we talked it all over, dreamed of what we wanted our lives to look like in our latter years, and prayed it through together. It has stuck with me since – I can't just hope to become more like Jesus; to be a wonderfully holy, kind, disciplined, loving OAP, I need to keep the goal in mind and work on all that now. Now that's a great talk. Can you think of a talk that has caused a change in you, or helped you to live differently? What made it so effective?

Developing Our Gift

So having looked at the importance and power of the Word, and words in general, perhaps we are some way to understanding why we should take our call to preach and teach seriously. We need to develop our gift, not neglect it – just as Paul urged Timothy. For many of us it might well be that teaching comes as part of the job we do in leading a church, in which case there is an even stronger imperative on us to pay attention to that gift.

In 1 Timothy 3:1-7, Paul details several qualities necessary for church leadership. In this list only one gift is mentioned – the ability to teach. All the other requirements are about character (hospitable, self-controlled, not a lover of money, etc.). This doesn't mean we have to be naturally gifted speakers before God can call us, or perfect communicators before

God can use us. Think about the twelve disciples; none of them were professional speakers. But, if we're called to leadership we need to work at our ability to teach. Whether there is a strong natural gift or not, we need to take seriously our responsibility to teach God's people.

We should do this because it's a biblical call, but also because time is precious. If we speak to a church of three hundred people for twenty minutes, that's a hundred listening hours or the equivalent of twelve full working days. In an age where time is one of the most precious commodities, this is a huge responsibility. We are taking up valuable hours and our commitment to excellence, as well as our diligent preparation, should reflect that.

This chapter was all by way of a foundation because from here on in, for the rest of the book, we're going to look very practically at how we can grow as effective communicators of God's Word.

Pause:

Can you think of a memorable talk you've heard and why it was so memorable (for good or for bad)? It's really good to identify who we admire as speakers, what holds our attention, what we remember, and why. It's good practice to keep reviewing this – when we hear something we love, and when we hear something we really don't, ask why. Learning to listen to talks critically in this way will be part of our development as communicators.

Interview

Canon J.John

J.John is an evangelist and preacher, speaking the world over and bringing God's truth to those inside the Church and out. He is king of the catchy, memorable line and always uses creative ways to help his audience connect with and retain his message. As well as being a great communicator, J.John is also generous in encouraging and resourcing others. It's not just about what God is doing through his particular ministry, but behind the scenes he is doing all he can, in big and small ways, to cheer on other speakers, including myself.

Why do we preach? What do you understand the purpose of preaching to be?

The classic definition of preaching is 'God speaking through personality'. It's a person being a channel of God's truth. And if God can speak through a donkey [Num. 22], he can speak through anything!

Have you always wanted to speak? When did you know it was part of your calling?

I got into evangelism and ministry naturally. The love of Christ compelled me, and then I discovered it was a gift as people pointed it out to me. Often you discover it's what you've been called to do once you're doing it.

Can you remember the first talk you ever gave? If so, how did it go?

I can: I was a student in London, and Andy Economides [now a speaker and author] and I were running the Christian Union. One of us would end up speaking when there wasn't a speaker available. We didn't know much, but we got up and spoke from our hearts. I didn't know all the apologetics, but I knew God loved me and the people I was speaking to. As I look back, it must have made the Lord smile – like when you look at your own child who tries something they can't quite accomplish – that's something we like as parents; the fact they're giving it a go. And in our vulnerabilities God blesses us more.

Is there any part of talk preparation or delivery that you've particularly had to work on?

Sometimes you spend so much time preparing a talk you forget to prepare yourself, and that is of utmost importance. The vehicle needs to be pure and humble. You craft the message but too often the messenger isn't prepared. 'Unless the Lord builds the house, its builders labour in vain' [Ps. 127:1], and I'm more conscious of this than ever. I love communicating, crafting, playing with words – my danger would be not being led by the Spirit of God. Also, I think I've become more conversational as I've grown older, like I'm having a chat with people, and now, I'm even more prepared to be vulnerable.

Who has inspired you as a speaker in the past, and who do you like to listen to now?

So many different preachers! There isn't one particular person. The first time I ever heard Eric Delve I was blown away – I had never heard Bible story-telling before then, I'd never seen preaching with drama presented in the way he did, and it totally inspired me. The preacher George Whitfield was known as the divine dramatist, and that's what struck me about Eric Delve's style.

People like Michael Green have stimulated my thinking. Joyce Meyer inspires me. And so many others have inspired me – not always well-known speakers, but ordinary men and women. It's the transparency, authenticity and vulnerability of people that makes the message powerful. And when people ask me about how to grow in their preaching gift, I encourage them to try and listen to as many different people as possible.

When you get to heaven God won't ask why you weren't more like someone else, but why you weren't more like you. Be inspired by other preachers, but don't lose the uniqueness of you. Draw from their style and technique, but don't lose yours. Going back to that classic definition of preaching – God speaking through personality – we must never lose that.

How do you prepare your talks, and what is your starting point?

I'm like a squirrel, picking up nuts all the time: collecting, and constantly thinking and praying. The Bible says that when the angel appeared to Mary, to foretell the coming of Jesus, 'Mary treasured up all these things and pondered them in her heart' [Luke 2:19], and similarly for me there is a period of pondering, considering and thinking. There is a gestation period – whether it's for a new sermon series or an individual talk – where I'm ruminating and marinating all the time. I keep trying to come up with new concepts, and when something strikes me I'll do research, I'll look for how that subject is being talked about in the media, what Bible stories reflect that idea. I gather lots of material and then begin to distil it down, siphoning off the material that isn't useful to the finished talk (which won't be wasted, as I will end up using it for other talks). Once I've done the gestating and distilling process, I will still need about three days to craft that into a finished talk. It's not that I spend three days in solid preparation – rather, I'll give it one day a week, so that by the time I get to the third week my thinking has developed. Then when I've given a talk once, I'll think about aspects I want to craft further.

What would you say is the most important element of a talk?

The person delivering it. Apart from that, the application. Exhortation without application leads to frustration. In other words, if you're encouraging people to, for example, read the Bible but don't teach them how, they will get frustrated. So we need to show *how*. Too often speakers stop before they get to the how. We need to cut back on the rest of the material in order to give space to application. Also feedback from others is so important – especially for a new talk. I welcome it rather than fear it.

What would you say makes a good talk, good and a bad talk, bad?

A good talk is concise, clear, convincing and colourful. A bad talk is when I don't know where the speaker's going; it has created confusion rather than clarity. And I think too often in charismatic circles we're not very good at communicating effectively. We sometimes feel we need to say more than we actually do. What's the one thing we want to communicate? We need to make it simple, which doesn't mean simplistic.

Can you think of any mistakes you've made, or problems you've had to overcome?

I think sometimes I've spoken for too long, and that hasn't been necessary. I think sometimes I have confused people because I haven't been clear. Also I've grown in confidence, so I can now do things I didn't do before – for example, the power of the pause. When I had less confidence, I would have worried that people would have thought I'd lost my place. I'm more in control now, less distracted or preoccupied.

Is there a particular verse or subject you love to speak on again and again?

Proclaiming the gospel is my primary calling – so for me it's introducing people to Jesus. I try to keep thinking and coming up with new ways of helping people see that path. The message is timeless, but the packaging or presentation isn't.

Do you have any top tips for engaging an audience?

I think it's a combination of things – it's important to be real, transparent and vulnerable, but I think you've also got to be authoritative. I think within all of that, eye contact is so important and if you don't have eye contact it can be difficult. That's why I don't like dark settings – despite people saying 'it creates ambience' – I would rather have all the lights on!

Don't show irritation: once you show that you're distracted by something it seems to grow, the audience pick up on it and you put yourself in a more vulnerable situation. There will always be distractions and things that don't go quite right, whether it's someone coughing, a baby crying, toddlers running around, teenagers texting, but God is God, and he is sovereign.

Be yourself. If you're yourself it's less stressful than trying to be somebody else, or trying to impress.

Also, very practically, don't be tied to your notes or to the lectern. As much as possible, I try and walk away from both. I don't memorize my stories, but I do run through them in my head or out loud beforehand. It may not be perfect on the day but it's more real than reading.

It's learning the balance – I will read quotes or Scripture or statistics, but I try to leave my notes as much as I can. That's hard work. I try to use tools so that I can remember and, more importantly, so that those listening can retain what I'm saying. So I come up with pegs for people to hang the message on, so that even if they can't remember the whole content there are reminders or triggers. This is an area we can all develop in, so that we help people remember what has been said. In the end let's always remember we do it all for Christ and with Christ – wow, that's a thought!

J.John lives in Chorleywood, Hertfordshire in England. He is married to Killy and they have three sons, Michael, Simeon and Benjamin. To date, he has completed thousands of speaking engagements at conferences, towns, cities and universities, in sixty-nine countries, on six continents. J.John has also authored several titles.

2.

The Very Beginning: Preparation Before Talk Preparation

You're going to write a talk and then you're going to give a talk. So where do you begin? Preparing a talk starts before we write anything down. Generally, it starts with the things God is brewing in our hearts, through reading the Bible, and in prayer.

Reading the Bible

When we speak we don't want to just be teaching good ideas, clever stories, or personal experience. Instead we want to bring that double-edged sword, the sharp word of God that has the power to change. The Word of God is the primary well that we have to draw from. As we go on, we'll be looking at the need for us to show how the truth of the Word is lived out in our own lives and the lives of others. Practical experience is hugely important, but our primary source and inspiration should be the Bible – not from the TV or a book, but first what we're reading in the Word. As my wise old dad puts it: we don't go to the Bible for what to speak on; we come from the Bible with what to speak on. In other words, we bring what God is already showing us – not turning to the Bible in a panic, searching for sermon fodder. Of course there will be exceptions to this rule, for example when we've been given a specific topic that needs addressing, but this idea of coming from the Bible is a really helpful principle.

Years ago, before I ever began to preach, I used to love stumbling across truths and gems in the Bible that I thought I was the only one to have ever discovered, then sharing these things with my friends or family. I used to write notes in my journal that were essentially talk outlines – I just didn't know it at the time. And this, coupled with the fact that I've always loved to talk, means it's probably not a surprise that communicating God's truth is now one of my primary passions. I remember when I first felt an inkling of being 'called' to teach. God made things very clear to me – that I was going to be a preacher, and that his call was going to take up a lot of my time and focus. However, I wasn't going to be released into it until I got deeper and more consistently into his Word. Although I'd loved discovering nuggets in the Bible, the truth was my reading of it was very erratic. Pretty much as soon as I got more consistently into his Word, people started to ask me to speak. Now that doesn't mean that we read the Bible in order to twist God's arm and get those speaking invitations flooding in, but it is our responsibility to be drawing our wisdom, truth and guidance from God's Word, to take nourishment from it for ourselves, first and foremost, and to pass on what he calls us to pass on. If we're not reading the Bible, we will have nothing worth passing on, our well will dry up, and we will not be moving forward with God in a way that enables us to teach his people.

Pause:

How consistently are you reading the Bible? If this is something you struggle to do on a regular basis, what help can you get? Do you need someone who will encourage you and cheer you on? Do you need to find a resource to help you get started?

Prayer

So we need to be reading the Bible. But before we start writing a talk we also need to be praying: 'God, what should I be speaking about? What is it that needs addressing? Please open up your Word to me and speak to me – give me something fresh for your people.' We need to pray for revelation from his Word. Some of the best teaching I've heard has been when someone has brought a totally fresh take on an old passage, or unpacked something in the Bible I haven't noticed before.

I once listened to a sermon online by a great teacher called Mike Erre. He was speaking about marriage and started right at the beginning in Genesis. He talked about the beauty of the poetry in the creation story, and the repetition of the line, 'And God saw it was good' (Gen. 1). Then he brought out the contrasting line: 'It is not good for the man to be alone' (Gen. 2:18), showing how in the perfection of creation the only thing that was not good was loneliness, and how God remedied this when he created Eve. Creation was good, loneliness was not. Over the years I've read Genesis loads of times and heard it spoken on probably just as often, but I've never seen that before. 'It is good', 'It is not good' – so simple, yet so brilliant.

We need to pray that God would reveal the hidden and unobvious truths in his Word to us, that we would see and understand at different levels, from different angles. It's fresh revelation that will captivate people with a love of God's Word, encouraging them to seek it out for themselves. It's also revelation that will cause people to turn to Jesus or open up to him. It is almost as though the freshness of his Word woos us and draws us closer to him.

So we need to be praying for revelation from the Bible, but we also need to pray for revelation of what needs to be addressed. We've looked at the fact that we come from the Bible with what to say, but it might also be that there is something that must be addressed for the sake of the needs of the church or the group we're speaking to, or we may have been set a particular passage or topic, either as a one-off or as part of a series. Then the prayer is how – how to communicate what needs to be taught. Sometimes there is no set theme or subject, so we need to seek the Lord for the 'what'. I often pray: 'Lord, I have no idea what these people need to hear, but you do.' It is good to spend time in prayer seeking God, asking what things are holding back this generation, or this group of people from going deeper in their relationship with him. What are the things that need addressing, and need God's truth and freedom in order to be overcome? This is often not just a prayer offered up in a moment but something God shows us over time, and when we feel as if he's spoken, then we go back to the Bible to see what his Word has to say on that issue.

In general, we don't have a clue what is going on in the lives of the people we're speaking to but God does, and he can help us reveal, craft and bring a word in season. So seek him for that word.

We can also pray for help in our communication. I'm encouraged both by the fear of Moses and the prayers of the apostles – I'm assured that I don't have to have what it takes, but I can ask God. When the Lord spoke to Moses from the burning bush about leading His people out of slavery, Moses had many fears and objections. One of them was about his inadequacy as a public communicator:

> 'O Lord, I have never been eloquent, neither in the past nor since you have spoken to your servant. I am slow of speech and tongue.'
> The Lord said to him, 'Who gave man his mouth? Who makes him deaf or mute? Who gives him sight or makes him blind? Is it not I, the Lord? Now go; I will help you speak and will teach you what to say.'
>
> Exod. 4:10–12

Then later in Acts 4:29, under very different circumstances, the believers prayed, 'Enable your servants to speak your word with great boldness.'

So we can pray when we feel inadequate, we can pray for God's help in finding the words. We can ask God to teach us how to do this.

And finally, as well as praying for his help and inspiration throughout every part of our preparation, we also need to pray for the anointing of God on our talk. Later on in this book, there is an interview with David and Mary Pytches. When I asked Mary what mistakes she has made in her preaching and teaching, she talked about the need to seek the anointing of God. And I realized I too often forget to ask God to anoint the message I'm preparing. Anointing speaks of holiness, something that has been set apart for God, something that has the favour of God on it. The Holy Spirit anoints people and messages, and while it is sometimes hard to precisely define, it's usually obvious when we see it. You know when you're hearing an anointed talk because it does the job – it goes beyond clever words and good insights. So much of what we will be looking at in this book becomes less important (though shouldn't be forgotten altogether) when our talks carry the anointing of the Holy Spirit. An anointed talk has that 'something more' – a sense of the presence of God, the electric fizz of God at work. We want our talks to carry this sense of his anointing – it's those talks that cut straight to the point, speak to the heart, open the eyes, and cause us to yearn for more of Jesus.

Before we have even written down a single word, we've begun our talk preparation through reading the Bible and seeking God for his help, guidance and anointing. This means that as we start to prepare in earnest, we kick off with whatever is already brewing in us, or that which God has laid on our hearts – the things that we've found in the Bible that have caused us to pause, or got our ears pricking up, or have made us excited. Often it is the truths that God is showing us personally, that could be good for other people to hear. For me one of my signature verses is from Matthew 10: 'What is whispered in your ear, proclaim from the roofs' (Matt. 10:27). This verse speaks to me, in part, of our role as teachers and preachers: God whispers something to us and we pass it on.

As we come to prepare our talks, let's begin with the Bible and recognize the importance of preparing in prayer. As we live life drawing from the well of the Bible and in prayer let's learn to recognize what God is growing in our hearts; what truth he is showing us that could have relevance for the wider Church community.

Pause:

What is brewing in your heart? What is God speaking to you about – in his Word and through his Spirit – at the moment?

3.

At the Starting-block – What Are You Going to Speak On?

The starting-block of writing a talk is often a scary place to be. Aaron Sorkin, writer of the TV series *The West Wing* and, more recently, the film *The Social Network*, once spoke of how much he loves writing but hates starting. He described the blank page as being very white and mocking him, implying his past success was merely accidental.

Facing the fear – the blank screen or piece of paper – is the first major hurdle we're going to need to jump in this challenging process of talk preparation. The next one is knowing how and where to begin.

As we saw in the last chapter, the best place to start (unless we've been given a specific topic or Bible passage) is with something God is showing us. Whatever the initial thought (and it may be no more than a thought), when it comes to working on it, it's a bit like looking for the end of the roll of sticky tape: you keep running your finger over it, and picking away when you feel an edge, until you are able to unravel more. Whatever God has led us to speak on, we need to spend time going through the (sometimes painful) process of waiting, mulling over and praying. We need to take our time picking away at the thought or inspiration, coming back to it again and again from lots of different angles. This will involve reading and re-reading Bible verses and passages, and noting anything that comes to mind, anything that strikes us or seems particularly important, interesting or relevant.

When the Starting Point Isn't Your Own

Many speakers don't have the luxury of being able to choose what to speak on – passages are set by someone else and you may even have to speak from an existing talk outline. This might sound easier, in that you don't have to come up with an idea, but it has its own challenges – being able to speak with passion on a subject that wasn't already 'in' you and making the topic your own can be tricky.

Speaking on a Set Bible Passage

Go about it in the same way as outlined in this chapter: read and re-read the passage, note down anything of interest, use study aids. The main difference is that you haven't had that initial spark, but as you keep reading, waiting and studying, something will eventually ignite in your heart or mind.

Speaking from a Talk Outline

This is where someone else has not only given you the topic or verse to speak on, but has also prepared bullet points for the structure of your talk. When this happens you will still need to ensure you personally read and study the set passage and get to grips with it yourself.

Even if you then don't or can't use that research, it will give you a confidence in the passage that might not be there otherwise. Once you've done this, you can then begin to expand on the points that have been set for you, ensuring you make it personal – use your own language, illustrations and reflections where you can.

At this stage, we need to study the Bible with an open mind, and not be too set on what we want to say (and therefore what we want the text to say), but allowing God's Word to speak to us as we read and pray. Our job is to serve God's Word, not make God's Word serve us.

We might do this initially by reading the passage or verse in many different translations – this might shed some light on it or suggest a direction we should take it. However, we shouldn't use a translation if it says something wildly different to a mainstream translation. A little rule or guideline I set myself is: I can only use an alternative translation if it enhances the meaning and helps draw it out, not if it seems to be saying something completely different to the other versions. This is important, I think, for our integrity as speakers.

Then, whatever theme or topic we want to speak on, we should spend time looking up all the ways God speaks about that issue in his Word, using a concordance and an online Bible tool, such as Biblegateway.com (an excellent site I couldn't live without, enabling one to search for keywords or by passage reference) to help. We need to spend time reading commentaries, Bible dictionaries, study Bibles, Bible handbooks, and anything else we can get our hands on. One book I love is *Unlocking the Bible* by David Pawson (Collins). Each chapter introduces a book of the Bible, draws out what the original context was and how it speaks to us today. It's a really easy read, a bit like reading a good sermon.

If we're speaking on an Old Testament character, it is good practice to check and see if they are referred to in the New Testament at all and if so, see whether this sheds any more light on their character or circumstances. A good example of this is all that Hebrews has to say about the Old Testament character of Abraham.

Doing all of this research early on will ensure we're speaking on what the text is actually saying and not what we want it to say. At this stage we may have to lay aside something we wanted to say if it's not properly supported.

How Long Should You Spend Preparing a Talk?

Talk preparation takes time. Time to ponder and pray, to study, to flesh out your content, to find illustrations, to focus on application. It all takes time, and it's important you give yourself enough space to do this well. Make time to chew things over and read. Carve time out in your diary (something I'm very bad at) to prepare talks, even when you don't know when you will next be giving one.

It's then at this beginning stage of our preparation that we begin to do some wider research on the topic. I've actually found it quite helpful to listen to other people's sermons on the same subject because I sometimes find a useful angle, or piece of information, or something I wouldn't have otherwise considered. We might want to do some research online, ask our friends, be on the lookout for how that subject is being talked about in the media, and think of examples from our own lives and the lives of others.

Once we've got our starting idea, we begin to brainstorm, writing down anything that comes to mind.

Depending on the way you think and process, it could be great to talk it out with one or two people. Sharing your thoughts out loud and bouncing them off others can be a great way to help clarify where you're going, and can bring out things you'd never think of on your own. If you're the sort of person who tucks quotes and illustrations away, see what you've got on this subject and how that inspires your preparation. At this stage we're not worrying about structure – this comes later. Instead, we are casting a wide net around our subject or theme, pooling all sorts of ideas and slants, many of which we may not end up using for this particular talk (but they won't be wasted as we can always use them in another talk).

At the Starting-blocks for *O Come Let Us Adore Him* (See Appendix 2)

My starting point for this talk was that it was Christmas. I was speaking on 22 December, so I really couldn't speak on anything other than the Christmas story. The trouble was I just couldn't find anything new to say. I spent hours and hours, over many days, reading and re-reading the two accounts of the nativity in Matthew and Luke. I also spent time on the internet, looking up facts and figures about the two people groups: the shepherds and the Magi. As I trawled through many web pages, I came across some facts about the wise men and suddenly it was like something clicked in my brain. It dawned on me how different the two groups of people were (even though they both ended up at the same destination – Jesus), and I started drawing comparisons.

So to get us off the starting-block, we're gathering all sorts of information and inspiration. Once we've done all the background work we look to see if one particular angle or point is emerging, and then we begin to develop it.

Pause:

Imagine you had to begin writing a talk this week. What would you speak about? What passage or theme or subject from the Bible is currently ticking away in you? What would you do next to begin developing that idea?

Why not begin to work on those ideas, to dig around those passages, even if you're not due to speak any time soon? Time spent in the Word will never be wasted, and it could be that you've got a good talk ready to go the next time you're asked to speak. If speaking is something you feel called to, then it's good for you to practise writing talks even if you're not doing lots of speaking at the moment.

Interview

Rachel Gardner

The first time I heard Rachel speak I was amazed at her ability to create a real atmosphere of intimacy – it felt as though we were a small group of friends together, even though, in reality, there was a crowd of several hundred. Her care for the individual translates to the crowd, and I love Rachel's energy, fun and passion. She is both wise and practical, bringing the Bible to life in grounded and relevant ways.

Why do we preach? What do you understand the purpose of preaching to be?

It's equipping God's people with the ability to 'listen both to the Word of God and listen to today's world' [John Stott][4] so good preaching should always feel very rooted in the Bible and rooted in the community. It should be about leading people towards understanding, not telling them what to do. And that equips them to live for Jesus in their everyday lives. Preaching should engage the senses, encouraging reflection as well as giving direct teaching. The listener should sense that a lot of preparation has gone into a talk, that it comes out of a lot of mulling and testing in the speaker's own life, and is therefore passing on wisdom. Preaching is less about information and more about formation; less about cramming brains with Bible trivia and more about helping people to be formed in the image of Christ. It's about leading them towards understanding.

As a speaker, I feel I must be very careful not to fill the space with words, but create space for God to fill. It's not about us saying that we have all the answers – God will reveal his truth, and my job is to create the environment for that to happen.

Have you always wanted to speak? When did you know it was part of your calling?

My calling is to communicate with people, and that happens on many levels. My main context is speaking at youth events. I'm a communicator rather than a teacher or preacher – because I love to communicate, it doesn't really matter if that's one-on-one or in front of a big group of people. I'm eager that when I communicate it would lead to a moment of enlightenment – 'Oh yeah, I get it!' – whether that's with an individual or a larger crowd.

So for me, public speaking has happened naturally because I've always enjoyed communicating. I get a lot of joy out of it (as well as nerves).

Can you remember the first talk you ever gave? If so, how did it go?

I really can! I was 17 and the head girl at my school – I gave the leaving speech. As I delivered it, I felt I gave something of myself, and I realized I had been able to say what the other pupils – my peers – were feeling. I was one of them and was able to summarize what we'd all been through. It was an incredible feeling. I wanted to communicate something that would help people mark the moment. And I loved it. I felt something in my spirit, something clicked, I think I felt God's pleasure – although that sounds a bit grand. It showed me possibilities – that when you communicate well you leave people feeling they've been understood.

Is there any part of talk preparation or delivery that you've particularly had to work on?

Yes – stopping! I find starting a talk easy, I enjoy developing an idea, but knowing when I've said enough is something I've found hard. I've really had to work on my endings, and learning how to be aware in the moment when I've said enough. A talk must finish well. So in working on this, I've had to give thought to my last paragraph, often writing it out in full. Experts say that people mainly remember the last ten minutes of a talk, so it had better be good!

Another thing I've had to work on is not apologizing for being there. I've found teaching those older than me more challenging, and have felt really tempted to justify why I'm there. Similarly, I've had to work on not being a people pleaser, and to choose to bring a message even if it might be hard for the listeners to receive.

Who has inspired you as a speaker in the past, and who do you like to listen to now?

I loved listening to John Stott because he paced himself so well. He's wasn't a 'glamorous' speaker, but was always so well prepared. In the UK we have lots of brilliant speakers – I love Steve Chalke's passion, and the compassion of Mike Pilavachi. Rob Bell is really creative about engaging people's brains and imaginations. While I was studying at the London School of Theology, I was really inspired by some of my lecturers because they could bring deep, intense doctrine to life. They taught me that God's Word lives. That there is a richness in God's Word that speaks for itself. You don't need to translate it for people, just lead them to understanding.

And last but not least, my dad – he's truly awesome, a wonderful Bible teacher. He draws people into what he's saying. I hope that I'm a bit like him.

How do you prepare your talks, and what is your starting point?

A starting point for me might be a Bible passage, a theme, something that has happened in the news. Then I write this initial idea in the middle of the page and begin to pack around that idea everything that might feed into it. Then I find the one point that I'm wanting to lead people towards and find lots of ways of reinforcing it. I always take into account different learning styles and I will invariably use PowerPoint – using images, rather than words, to create associations. I will always work into my talks space for reflection. I do have a pretty tried and tested structure that I work to most of the time.

What would you say is the most important element of a talk?

Our integrity as speakers – it's important that we never speak beyond what we have been prepared to live out.

I feel, in communication with young people, that I need to have allowed God's Word to have shaped me before I take it anywhere else. This is hard. It's not that we have to be perfect, but there does need to be integrity and humility so that a talk is not just our good idea, but something that God is working out in us. People – especially young people – will smell hypocrisy a mile off.

What would you say makes a good talk, good and a bad talk, bad?

A bad talk is like a cheap chicken burger that clogs you up for a while but has no long-lasting goodness. Whereas a good talk is like a top-class curry that keeps on repeating on you. A good talk is aspirational, full of hope. It opens up ideas and possibilities, and leads you to understanding – making you think and work at an idea for yourself as a listener. And also, a good talk is where there is some intimacy between the speaker and audience.

A bad talk has a lot to do with the speaker's attitude, and not being aware of who they're speaking to. A speaker needs to find out who their audience is – even the best talk is no good if it doesn't take into account the culture of the listeners. If I'm speaking to a bunch of young people that I've never met before, I will always get to the venue in time to make some kind of physical contact with them (shaking hands, etc.) – this shows them respect, and helps me connect with them.

Can you think of any mistakes you've made, or problems you've had to overcome?

There have been times where in my planning I go off on one and don't stick to my brief. The times when I've felt I've missed the point are when I've prepared in the wrong way (which is worse than being underprepared). You can be spontaneous if you know what you're doing – if you don't' know where you're going that can make your listener feel nervous, and then they aren't free to listen to you. If you want to be spontaneous, know where you're going.

   Also, if I don't eat enough beforehand I get light-headed, and I will waffle and go off on one – and no one can stop you once you're up there!

Is there a particular verse or subject you love to speak on again and again?

I love talking about hope and Jesus' transformational power, which changes us and heals our hearts. In Romans 4:18 Paul writes, 'Against all hope, Abraham in hope, believed'. Doesn't this say so much? It's beautiful because it sounds good, and it is good.

Do you have any top tips for engaging an audience?

Enjoy your space, enjoy your voice, enjoy the heart that God has stirred in you, and enjoy the message he has asked you to pass on. And if people aren't looking at you, move towards the front, stand very still and talk quite quietly. This engages curiosity and it will help draw people to you.

Rachel is co-founder and director of the Romance Academy, a revolutionary relationships project that builds young people's self-esteem, enhanced by sexual delay. Her work involves training youth workers and peer educators across the UK to deliver holistic relationship and sex education programmes in schools and community centres. Rachel also runs Romance Academy projects in her local area and teaches in secondary schools in north London. She is married to Jason and lives in Harrow, London where they are on the leadership team of a missional church for teenagers and young adults. Rachel is author of Cherished: Boys, Bodies and Becoming a Girl of Gold *(IVP) and co-author of* Rise: One Way, One Life, One Master *(IVP)*

4.

The Meat* – Content

You've waited, you've pondered and you have an idea. Like a newly conceived foetus, it is probably fairly unformed and you don't have a clue what it will look like when it's full grown, but at least it's there. So how do you move from this little idea to a fully-formed talk?

Keeping the Content Biblical

The starting point is to make sure the Bible is always central to what we're saying and not just tag it on at the end, or even throw in a random verse for the sake of it. My personal litmus test is: if I could give a talk in a school assembly then it hasn't got enough Bible in it for a church setting. Without the Bible, our sermons will simply expound good morals or teach positive life skills, which while helpful and perhaps interesting, are not the main purpose of preaching.

So we're coming from the Bible as we build our content. We have identified the passage, theme or character that we want to speak on. As we ponder and pray, read and research, we should

---

* Vegetarian option available

be asking ourselves two important questions about the Bible passage: 'What did it mean?' and 'What does it mean?' The technical terms for these two words are exegesis and hermeneutics. Simply put, exegesis is digging into what the passage was actually saying at the time it was recorded, and looking at the clues that lie in and around the written text. Hermeneutics is the wider research we do to help us apply the passage to people today. Exegesis is about explanation – what did it mean then, what was happening in the original context, what led up to that story, event or verse? Hermeneutics is about interpretation – what does the passage have to say to us today?

The 'What did it mean?' and 'What does it mean?' questions should always be considered. In the past I've been bad at prioritizing the first of the two, and have typically headed straight for the interpretation. But, as I'm learning, interpretation is always strengthened by first setting the context. Depending on the talk we're giving, we'll use the answer to these questions to varying degrees. Some talks merely nod at the former and focus on the latter, but both will inform our material and direction. If we're using a Bible story to speak on a theme, we should consider first explaining and teaching the actual story, setting it in context ('What did it mean?') before giving it a wider application to our lives, even if this is done very briefly. We draw out the 'What did it mean?' question before focusing on the 'What does it mean?' application. I think this can be an important step that we're sometimes too quick to miss out. When we provide a strong context, our teaching will feel so much more grounded in the truth. We won't be talking about a nice concept that we've dreamt up (and trying to use the Bible to back up our own good ideas). Instead, in setting a context, we're showing how our teaching – our hermeneutic – has been drawn from the original story.

As we're examining the text in our preparation, we should be looking for and asking God to show us fresh insights into his Word. Sometimes these jump out as we're doing our exegetical research. When we understand something more of the culture, language, or original situation, it brings a revelation for us today. If we can look at a passage and find something that most people won't know, that's going to get their attention.

Having said this, not everything we say has to be new or stunningly fresh – what we are basing our content on is very old, thousands of years old. We all need to be reminded of old truths and there will often be new believers or non-Christians at church who won't have heard it before – so don't worry about bringing out old themes from time to time. However, our aim should still be to bring this out in such a way as to engage our audience – how can I talk about an old truth in an original way?

Giving the Gospel

It is a good thing to regularly weave the gospel message into our preaching, wherever our content lends itself to this. It doesn't need to be a full unpacking of our sin, and Jesus' death and resurrection, forgiveness, grace and mercy – although we should be doing this from time to time. Sometimes giving the highlights as part of your talk will be enough. It is also good to regularly give opportunity for people who don't know Jesus to come into relationship with him. This can be as simple as saying at the end of your talk, 'Perhaps you don't yet know this Jesus I've been talking about. If you would like to know more, come and chat to me at the end.' (Or whatever is appropriate in your context). It might be that no one becomes a Christian (as far as you know), but the very worst that can happen is that a non-Christian sees the relevance of your talk to them, and a Christian is reminded that they could be inviting their non-Christian friends to church.

It is important to never assume that everyone in our audience knows what we're talking about or has pre-existing knowledge of the Bible, and its themes and characters. If we're going to refer to a Bible story or person in passing then we should give enough detail so that everyone knows who or what we're referring to. A simple sentence or two will probably be sufficient to include everyone and ensure we're all on the same page.

As we unpack our passage we should make sure we give enough detail so that people who haven't been Christians for years can come on board, and those that have are reminded of what's going on. There are many familiar passages and stories in the Bible with confusing elements that even mature Christians might just skip over. So giving background, context and explanation will help them too. By setting the context we will ensure that everyone is included in our talk, and that it's not just accessible for someone who has read their Bible from cover to cover, or grown up attending Sunday school.

In the same way, if we're not going to speak on a whole story, but are just going to focus on a few verses, then we should make sure we give a good and brief overview first, rather than diving in halfway through the story and expecting people to be on the same page as us. It's important we don't labour this overview, but do it concisely and interestingly, without dawdling.

Different people have different views on whether or not it's acceptable to take Scripture out of context – that is to pull a verse out from the original setting. Personally, I think if we are going to do this we should check that the truth of the verses remains even when we are taking it out of context. I once did a talk entitled, *Passing it on is Part of Our Purpose as People Who Belong to God* (it was an experimental title, in hindsight a few too many Ps). As part of this talk, I wanted to show that passing on God's love, truth, good news is a biblical principle. One of the tools I used to do this was a verse from 1 Corinthians: 'For I received from the Lord what I also passed on to you' (1 Cor. 11:23). The specific context for this verse is around the sharing of the Lord's Supper. However, I felt comfortable using it because Paul uses this phrase (or something similar) a few different times, in different ways, and because the idea that we freely receive, so we freely give (Matt. 10:8) is a biblical principle that I drew out in the rest of the talk. If we do decide to use a verse that has been slightly pulled away from its original framework, then it's a good idea to confess that this is what we've done so that people aren't left insecure about the truth they've received.

Get the Gear

There are certain books and resources you can get to help you prepare a sound and well-researched talk. If nothing else you should certainly start with:

- Study Bible
- Bible Commentary
- Bible Dictionary
- Access to the internet (biblegateway.com is a great resource)

Bringing Bible Stories to Life

We should think of different ways to bring the verse, passage or story to life. This can involve using visuals, a video, illustrations, or even getting someone else to read the passage out loud (more on this in a later chapter). We can also make the Bible content more real for the audience by making observations, explaining traditions or casting light on language used. It's a great idea to find ways to make the Bible pictures, stories or characters meaningful and relatable to today because this will help people connect with and remember that the Bible is fact not fiction, and is full of real people and situations. I heard a talk on the character of Zacchaeus recently where the speaker painted a picture of Zach as a biblical Danny Devito (the little fat actor from the 1990s – if you're too young to remember him, check him out online), a cheeky chappy with an exposed hairy chest, sporting garish gold jewellery. I was amazed at how instantly having a mental picture of Zacchaeus reconnected me to a story I've known as long as I can remember, and it really helped bring to life what was being taught.

That said, I do think we need to be careful when using humour around the Bible. Humour aimed at an individual character and which brings a story to life is fantastic; there are lots of places in the Bible where this is possible – just look at the life and one-liners of Peter for a start. But I think we should avoid a humour that shows, or even gives the impression of, disrespect for God's living and active Word. Poking fun at people in the Bible is fine, but poking fun at the Bible itself is another matter. As preachers and teachers we want people to love God's Word, and to respect it and turn to it. Undermining it with our humour will not help that goal.

The message of the Bible should be running through our talks, one way or another, but we should be careful not to litter what we say with too many Bible passages just to show that the talk is Bible-based. The second time I spoke at my church I chose the theme of worship which is something I am particularly passionate about. I wanted the talk to be biblical, so I included many references to worship throughout the Old and New Testament. I recently found that talk – now several years old – on my computer and counted thirty-seven Bible passages in it, many used back-to-back. Thankfully, at the time someone pointed out that this was perhaps a little too much to take in one sitting, and I took that feedback on board. It's better to use one or two passages, and use them well, than include a long list of verses that will overload people and not allow enough space for the application to be drawn out. It is better for the audience to understand one passage than be confused about lots. People won't be able to take it in if you use too many, and will struggle to focus. If we've already got a strong Bible passage in a talk, then a good way of including more of the Bible without too many references is to include it in the body of the talk, for example: 'The truth is all of us have sinned, and all of us fall short of the glory of God, but the good news is . . .' So we're preaching the Bible instead of quoting it. It's also sensible to avoid tackling more than one tough passage in a talk, as it will be too much for people to take in, unless the talk is a seminar, where you will go into more detail on a specific subject and people have come prepared for that level of information.

How to Present the Bible

Here are some practical tips on using the Bible in the delivery of your talk:

* When quoting from the Bible, don't leave your audience wondering why a passage has been used or assume its inclusion in a talk is self-explanatory.
* So when reading the Bible ensure you draw out why you've used the passage – how does it inform what you're looking at?
* If we're speaking on a specific passage it can be good to refer to other times in the Bible where God acted in a similar way, or where there is teaching on a similar theme. It's great for people to see and hear that what you're talking about is not a one-off.

- People should leave church knowing they've heard from the Word of God, so although it may sound obvious, it is a good idea to make sure you actually read from the Bible and not just allude to it. If you can get them to get their Bibles out, even better.
- If you are going to use a translation different to the one that is normally used by the church, it's helpful to let the congregation know that, and why.
- If you want to tell a long Bible story then think about telling some of it in story form: you don't necessarily need to read a whole chapter – you might want to sketch some bits as a paraphrase, tell other parts in a lot of detail, and read other sections directly from the Bible. This will help bring the passage to life and keep it interesting, skipping over any parts that aren't relevant to what you're saying.
- Similarly, if you need to read a long passage, pause to comment, explain words or circumstances. If you interrupt yourself from time to time it will help keep people's interest.
- If you're going to be using a long passage, it's worth considering asking someone else to read, for a change of voice. Whoever is doing the reading, make sure they do so in an engaging way that brings the passage to life.
- If you are referring back to a passage you read earlier in the talk, quote it again. The content of the Bible passage is at the forefront of your mind because you're speaking on it, but most people will need reminding.
- Check in advance that your Scripture references are right – so that when you tell the congregation that John 3:16 says, 'For God so loved the world' it's actually true. And not, 'This is how we know what love is: Jesus Christ laid down his life for us', which is 1 John 3:16.
- It's a good idea to mark the correct page in the Bible in advance so you can go straight to it rather than hunting about for it and interrupting the flow. Alternatively, if you are someone who writes your talk in full – rather than note

form – then think about simply typing the passage directly into your talk notes.
• If at all possible, it's great to be able to put the passage up in front of your audience – most churches have the technical capabilities to do this (even if it's a neatly-written overhead projector slide). People are much more likely to take in and remember what they see alongside what they hear, and keeping the passage in front of them will help them follow you as you work through it, if that's what you are doing.

A final note to conclude this section: if you speak regularly, think about varying the way you use the Bible in your talks. This will not only add variety to the way you focus on the Bible, but will also affect the way you choose to structure your talk, which we will be looking at in a later chapter. Here are some examples:

• Unpacking a passage line by line, or verse by verse
• Focusing on one verse
• Speaking on a character
• Looking at a biblical theme, for example, love or forgiveness
• Unpacking a story, for example, the raising of Lazarus
• Preaching on a whole book of the Bible

Pause:

Do you find yourself preparing the same type of talk again and again, i.e. always building your content around a passage, or keyword, or aspect of God's character? What different approach to your content could you think about trying next time?

Building Content

Having looked at how to use the Bible, here are some thoughts on how to prepare and present the content of our talks:

* As you work on your content, keep reviewing it to make sure it is clear. The best theology is communicated in such a way that it doesn't feel like arduous learning (American speaker, pastor and author, Louie Giglio, is a master of this). When my dad was a pastor there was an 18-year-old girl, Irene, in our church who was just learning to read and write. One of Dad's aims when writing his sermon was to communicate in such a way as not to make Irene frown. If she did, it meant he had used a word or concept she didn't understand and it needed to be explained. He still thinks of Irene now, thirty years on, to ensure his talks are clear. We need to find ways of keeping our talks simple and accessible without being basic or shallow.
* Make sure your content reflects what you are trying to say. You've heard of 'put your money where your mouth is'. Well, in preaching, you need to put your 'material where your point is'. In other words, spend time developing your content around what you actually want to say. Don't get sidetracked.
* It can be really helpful to check with someone else to see if what you've got in your heart and head is actually coming across in your material. Because you've been immersed in this topic for days, weeks, perhaps even months you'll know exactly what you mean, but someone else might not. So get someone else to check things over before you finish a talk, and certainly before you give it.
* Don't overly repeat or labour a point. Do it well, then move on. And when you've said what you want to say, stop.

- Remove unnecessary details that will clutter and detract from what you're saying, e.g. 'So I thought I would speak this morning on prayer. But as I prayed a bit more I thought that maybe instead I should speak on worship. And then as I was watching the news something occurred to me, and having then read my daily Bible-reading notes, I knew I should speak on intercession.' Instead you could simply say, 'This morning I want us to look together at intercession – what it is, why we do it and how we do it.'

- Know who you're speaking to. Never write for a faceless crowd, but instead be thinking of your content in terms of your audience: are you speaking to old or young, married or not, Christian or not? The chances are it will always be a mixture, but have that in mind as you write and prepare.

Bringing a Tough Word

Sometimes we may feel, for one reason or another, that we need to bring a word of challenge or rebuke. These can be hard messages to give as they aren't usually what people want to hear. If God leads us to do this, we need to weigh it up, pray some more and seek advice, but we shouldn't shy away from it. It isn't our job to make people feel warm and fuzzy; it's our job to point people to Jesus. So if you need to bring a challenge, here are a few ideas of how to tackle this:

- Make sure you celebrate what is good more than you criticize what is bad. I once heard someone say that we should dangle a carrot rather than beat with a stick. Talk about and give testimonies of the good things that happen when we respond well to the particular issue, and show people what God loves and praises.

- Ensure there are moments of lightness, so that the whole talk isn't heavy.
- Speak as a pastor, showing your concern and love, rather than anger or frustration.
- It will be more important than ever to address the audience as 'we' rather than 'you'. Include yourself as a recipient of the challenge.
- Don't leave people with a burden on their shoulders; leave them with Jesus. Remind them of his strength, his grace, his power, etc. Leave them looking to him and leaning on him.

Content in *O Come Let Us Adore Him*

Before I drew out the comparisons between the shepherds and the Magi, I knew I would have to tell their stories. I did this by reading the accounts from the Gospels, interrupting myself along the way to give background and insights. It probably wasn't the most in-depth analysis of the passages – and that wasn't my aim – I just wanted to be sure that the story was fresh and clear in people's minds.

I also worked hard to bring the shepherds and the Magi to life, so they weren't just characters we've read about, but real people who met God. This meant we were all on the same secure foundation for my reflections, which came in the second half of the talk.

In hindsight, it definitely needed cleaning up in places. There are quite a few references to 'and then I read in my commentary/found out/thought about'. Sentences like these don't strengthen a talk, but clutter it up unnecessarily.

Know Your Key Themes

The whole of the Word of God needs to be preached, but over time speakers often find they have one or two dominant or recurring themes in their teaching; subjects they come back to and want to communicate again and again. This is especially good if we work in team, as there will then be a natural balance. While most of us won't get to speak on those one or two things all the time, it's not a bad thing to return to our strengths and passions. There is often a real authority and anointing when we do this, so it's quite helpful if we know what they are. For example, one of my key themes would be discovering the truth of who we are in God. I can work just as hard on topics of a different nature, but there is often something special in my communication when I talk on this issue. It is good for us to remember that some of the things God has put on our heart are probably not on the hearts of others in the same way. As we build and develop our content, let us remember to play to our strengths.

Finally, when we speak we should be looking to bring content that would both warm the heart and inform the mind. In Hebrews 8:10 the writer quotes a passage from Jeremiah 31:33: 'I will put my laws in their minds and write them on their hearts.' Hebrews 10:16 quotes the same passage, with a slight difference: 'I will put my laws in their hearts, and I will write them on their minds.' Some of us receive truth first in our minds and then it eventually ends up in our hearts. For others, it's the other way round. Either way God in his Word has got it covered, and our aim as communicators should be to speak truth and grace to both the heart and mind.

Pause:

Do you know what your theme(s) in preaching might be? Even if you've never given a talk, think about the themes, issues or subjects that are closest to your heart.

5.

Stick to It: Finding and Developing Your Main Focus

After thinking about the overall content we need to begin to take our preparation a stage further, to home in on what we actually want to communicate. As you work on the content by studying the Bible and using other resources, you will find you get to the stage where you have a pretty good idea of what you want to say, of where you (roughly) want the talk to go. At this stage, it's time to pin your talk down to one main focus, and ensure you begin to work out how to communicate that principal idea with clarity.

Why Do We Need to Find a Main Focus?

Firstly, we need to look more fundamentally at why we should identify one focus when we may have been used to a very different speaking model. (The traditional three-point sermon is often more like the three-sermon sermon.)

We want people to do more than just be engaged in our talks: we want them to remember what we have said, but even more than this we want them to be changed by the truth of God's Word. When I'm dissatisfied with my life I come up with a long list of the many things I'm going to change. A classic time for this is over New Year, when we come up with resolutions for the coming months. So far, I have never managed to set myself just one challenge, there are always about ten: exercise more, rest more, read more, lose weight, stop biting my nails, get out into nature more, pray more, read my Bible more . . . and of course with several bull's-eyes to aim for, I miss all of them, and end up feeling guilty or discouraged, or both. If only I could learn to go for one target at a time.

It's potentially the same with our preaching. If we throw out loads of ideas for people to take away with them, the chances are they won't remember or act on any of them. This doesn't mean that in our talk we only say one thing – we may have five or six insights, components or aspects to share. But all these insights should point to the one focus.

I recently came across a sermon on the internet, and as I read it I began to realize that there were several points emerging in a strange yet clever pattern. Intrigued, I copied the document into a Word file and got rid of most of the material until all I was left with were the author's headings. I was amazed. What I saw before me was an obsession with alliteration. Each of the three main points (all beginning with R and P) were broken down further with three more sub-points, many of which were then broken down yet further, and rather cleverly, most of those began with the same letters – there were twenty-three points in total. By now you may well be quite confused. I know I was! As I read, I couldn't imagine what it would be like to listen to such a complicated talk, to try to take it in, let alone digest and put it into action later.

When preparing a talk we must remember that there is a goal in mind. The goal is not to impart as much information as possible in a twenty-minute time frame. The goal is not to dazzle our listeners with our clever words or imaginative structure. The goal may vary slightly from person to person, and from talk to talk, but I would suggest in general, our goal is to reveal God and his truth.

We work hard at our talks so that we can bring a revelation from God's Word and so that people will hear, understand, lean on God, and become more like him as a result. With this being the case, we want people to be able to follow what we've said, remember what we've said and then live out of the truth of what we've said. If this is going to happen, we need to ensure that our talks are clear, simple (although that doesn't have to mean basic) and easy to follow.

One great way of doing this is finding and sticking to one thing we want to communicate.

Don't Say What You're Not Going to Say

It can be very frustrating to waste time hearing a speaker say, 'I'm not going to speak on this today' – unless there is something obvious that is not going to be covered and it's more distracting not to allude to it. There is sometime a temptation to make ourselves look better and more competent by showing that we are aware of what we're not talking about, and we need to resist this as it comes from fear of people (and not God). Similarly, be wary of raising a question and leaving it unanswered. For example, 'How do we do this?', unless you deliberately want to raise tension and will answer the question later on.

Finding and Developing Our Main Focus

So how do we do this? One way of identifying a central focus is to learn to spot that place in our preparation when we get particularly excited or passionate – the material that more easily flows, the stuff we want to preach to everyone we meet, including the neighbours' cat. The chances are that's it, that's our main thing.

Another way is to look for the common thread in our ponderings, or the unifying thought that ties much of our preparation together. Sometimes we will know where our focus is going to be before we even begin to prepare, sometimes it develops as we write a talk, and sometimes it ends up being totally different to what we thought it was going to be. Having said that, we need to try to identify our main focus sooner rather than later. It's easy to get stuck into writing reams and reams, and then at some point work out what it is we really want to say. So the sooner we can identify the key message, the better.

We should try asking ourselves what we actually want to communicate. It sounds obvious, but so often people don't think it through, or leave it as a woolly, general idea. Too frequently a speaker knows what he or she wants to say, but fails to get that across, leaving the listeners unclear what that last thirty minutes of their life was all about. So the main emphasis of what we want to communicate needs to be firmed up and clarified, and then we should ask ourselves: 'What is my bottom line; the one thing I'd love God to help me get across, the one thing I'd love people to go away with?'

And then we need to ask ourselves: 'Can I describe my talk, or the emphasis of my talk, in one sentence?' I would say this is an important step, because if we can't be sure what it is we want to say, no one else will be either. Having said this, don't be too worried if you can't summarize succinctly early on in your preparation, just make sure you keep coming back to those questions throughout your work. I always imagine that people are hanging out on a Sunday, perhaps over Sunday lunch, or drinks that evening. Some of the group were at church and some weren't. I imagine one person asking another, 'Who spoke at church today, what was the sermon on?' And then my aim is always that the person responding would be able to easily and briefly sum up what I said. Holding this scenario in my mind helps me clarify and define the major thrust of my talk. This isn't necessarily a catchy statement, it's just a one-sentence summary of the entire talk. For example:

- Don't just live with a negative self-image – do something about it.
- Persevere: keep going when things are tough.
- There's always meat in the Word even when it doesn't seem obvious.

As our principal emphasis becomes clear, we need to ensure that it is central to every other bit of preparation and hard work we do, and every Bible passage, illustration and quote we use. Imagine your talk is a flower. In the centre is your main focus, every petal that comes off the centre must relate back to the core focus. Everything should hang off and return to that central idea, never moving far away from it. Here is an example of a talk I wrote on weakness and failure:

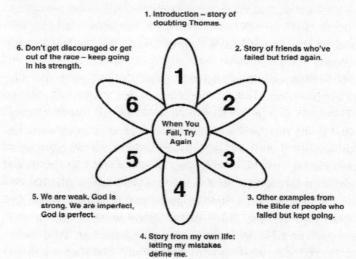

1. Introduction – story of doubting Thomas.

2. Story of friends who've failed but tried again.

3. Other examples from the Bible of people who failed but kept going.

4. Story from my own life: letting my mistakes define me.

5. We are weak, God is strong. We are imperfect, God is perfect.

6. Don't get discouraged or get out of the race – keep going in his strength.

When You Fall, Try Again

'When You Fail, Try Again' is the centre of the flower because it is the main focus of the talk. The petals are the main elements of the talk:

1. Introduction – story of doubting Thomas.
2. Story of friends who've failed but tried again.
3. Other examples from the Bible of people who failed but kept going.
4. Story from my own life: letting my mistakes define me.
5. We are weak, God is strong. We are imperfect, God is perfect.
6. Don't get discouraged or get out of the race – keep going in his strength.

As you can see, there are several points, but one focus. Every bit of content in a talk ought to serve the one, central theme. Everything else we say should expand, teach, illustrate and unpack it. The aim is that we never wander too far away from the main focus. So, once you've found that one thing, be disciplined in getting rid of anything that doesn't fit with it. It may be that you have been working on this idea as one of three – but now consider making it the focus. There is nothing worse than sitting through thirty minutes of waffle and feeling like the speaker only got to the good stuff in the last ten minutes. Discard the material that doesn't serve your ultimate purpose. There have been times when I've ditched about half of a talk, but nothing is wasted – if you don't use it in this talk you'll use it in another. Just be sure you keep it. Cut and paste it into another document, or file the pieces of paper somewhere where you can come back to them. The material you get rid of will most certainly have shaped and strengthened your presentation. When giving a talk we give the tip of the iceberg. There is a whole lot more material under the water that is not seen but is part of the process, and often it's the hard work and the homework we did that gives weight to what is actually presented. A friend of mine once compared this process to preparing a good meal. If a dinner guest appreciates your cooking, the chances are they won't be able to name every ingredient you've used, they just enjoy the end result. In the same way every ingredient – every piece of research and reading – isn't always obvious in our talks, but they help us present a great end result. So we need to have the discipline and the courage to leave out anything that doesn't fit our core focus:

- Don't worry if narrowing your focus feels unnatural to begin with. Initially, it can be a bit scary ('Will I have enough to say?') and a bit simplistic ('Shouldn't I be delivering more than one thing?'). Just remember there is a goal in your preaching, and keeping it simple means we are much more likely to hit that target.

- If you're struggling to identify your one thing, try saying out loud what you'd love God to do through the talk. Not only does this help define your bottom line, it also begins to connect you to your purpose in giving the talk, which helps talk preparation feel less arduous. (Inevitably at some point in your preparation, it will feel like wading through treacle – so be prepared and don't worry if this happens).

- Once you've established your central aim, try writing that main focus on every page of your notes. This will serve as a helpful reminder to not wander away from it as you write. Alternatively, stick the picture of the flower in front of you, and keep asking yourself does this story, this illustration, this application serve and hang off the key point?

- It can also be a good thing to give your talk a title, or a one-sentence summary. This doesn't mean it can't change – in fact it often does – but it's good to begin pinning down where you want to go.

Be Consistent with Your Language

If you are unpacking your material through the use of analogy, use consistent language for ultimate clarity. Think about Paul's picture of the armour of God in Ephesians 6. Having said, 'Put on the full armour of God' (Eph. 6:11) he then goes on to talk about breastplates, helmets and swords. His language is consistent with the 'armour' analogy.

You might want to think about finding ways to keep repeating your one thing in the content of your talk. I tried this once after reading advice in a great book called *Communicating for a Change* by Andy Stanley (Multnomah Books). He suggests coming up with a memorable well-crafted line at some point in a talk to help people remember what you've said. At the time I was writing a talk about how all of us who are Christians are called to pass on the good news of Jesus. When I read the book I thought I'd give it a go, so I came up with the highly contrived title I referred to in the previous chapter: *Passing it on is Part of Our Purpose* as *People Who Belong to God*. I repeated this line over and over in my talk. In hindsight, I wonder if having the sentence so full of Ps made it a little over the top (and I had trouble not spitting on the front row), but the feedback I had that week suggested to me that more people than usual had understood and remembered what I'd been talking about.

Using this tool will help people remember the key message, and they'll be able to take it away with them. Alternatively, rather than using the same phrase, think of different ways of saying the same thing, so you're repeating your main idea, but driving it home in lots of forms.

Finally, having identified your main focus, go through your notes and make sure you've said it. Decide what you want to communicate and then communicate it, and nothing else.

The Main Focus of *O Come Let Us Adore Him*

The initial focus of this talk was the Christmas story itself, and the main focus was worship: whether we are more like the Magi or more like the shepherds we are still to draw close to God.

Pause:

If you've given a talk recently, go back and review it in the light of this chapter. Did you focus on one thing or many things? Would it have been obvious to your listeners what you wanted them to grasp and take away with them? If not, how could you do it differently another time?

The next time you're listening to someone else speak, see if you summarize in one sentence what they are speaking on. If they outlined what they wanted to say at the start, did they then do it? If they had several points to their talk, could they have discarded other points in order to focus on one thing? If you were able to spot a main focus, what tools did they use to communicate this?

Interview

Andy Croft

I was with Andy when he gave one of his early talks. It was fine, but it wasn't great. But now, he is a fantastic communicator, bringing the Bible to life with real clarity. He has a gift for taking theology and complicated ideas and communicating them with simplicity, in a very relevant and accessible way, something which is so hard to do. Andy has been very committed to learning and growing in his speaking gift, and I always love hearing whatever he has to say.

Why do we preach? What do you understand the purpose of preaching to be?

The purpose of preaching is to communicate the love of God in a language people's hearts understand. God's love is so utterly wonderful, and our human worldviews so limited and crude, that we often struggle to receive and accept who he is, what he's done and what that means for us. The role of the preacher is to help us understand this. By 'understand', I mean, not just being filled with information, but developing in our hearts, minds and souls a greater knowledge of the one who loves us, and thus a deeper level of relationship with him.

Have you always wanted to speak? When did you know it was part of your calling?

Growing up, I never really considered the idea. I did a short talk in my school chapel once (but only because the chaplain asked me in front of some of my mates and I didn't want to back down). When I did my gap year with Soul Survivor, I never volunteered to speak because the thought of writing a talk stressed me out. Eventually, I was 'asked' (they made me). I said yes – and promptly got stressed.

It was around this time I began to get a sense that this was what I was called to do – one giveaway was the fact that even though I didn't enjoy the whole process, I didn't quit. If I hadn't thought God was telling me to do it, I definitely would have. I still get stressed, but I've also started to really enjoy the fact that I actually get to do this as a living – another telltale sign that I think I'm called to do it.

I really enjoy studying and discovering things about God's Word I'd never realized before, and I also love communicating the stuff that excites me to others. I'm not too bothered about whether it excites them – so long as they shut up and listen (another sign I'm made to preach!).

Can you remember the first talk you ever gave? If so, how did it go?

I was 17, and it was that time in my school chapel. The talk was five minutes long. I woke up that morning at 4 a.m., sweating, and couldn't get back to sleep. In the end the talk seemed to go alright – I just said my little point and got out of there. Afterwards, of course, I acted like I hadn't been nervous at all.

Is there any part of talk preparation or delivery that you've particularly had to work on?

In terms of delivery, two mistakes I often make, but am trying to rectify are, firstly, coming across too teacher-like – this would involve a me-teaching-you-listening approach. It's characterized by lots of uses of the word 'you', as opposed to 'us': 'You might find this helpful. . .', 'You might not realize. . .' It can also sometimes involve a slight vibe of 'I know lots and lots, and I'm sharing some of my vast amount of knowledge with you'. The issues of me being a little arrogant aside, on a practical, communications level, people always respond much better when we go on a journey of discovery together, rather than them sitting there while I tell them something. More often than not I aim for the more truthful, 'I didn't realize this, but then found out. . .' Part of this is remembering we're not communicating information but revelation: 'I'd never seen this before'; 'Isn't this amazing?'

Another mistake is trying too hard. I went through a phase of listening to lots of speakers who could communicate loudly and passionately, and I wished I could be a bit more like that. Not long after I was doing a seminar for guys entitled, 'Man Up', and it was all about what it is to be a man following Jesus. I spent the whole seminar shouting at these poor teenage guys in what I thought was a passionate and inspiring way. Afterwards my good friend told me I just sounded angry. He pointed out to me that shouting at people is not always the best way to excite them. One of the most valuable lessons I've learned about communication is that there's a passion that excludes people and a passion that includes people. This will look different for different preachers, but for me it often involves understating a point, and suggesting or imagining with my language, rather than shouting and ordering.

Who has inspired you as a speaker in the past, and who do you like to listen to now?

John Wimber – not that I've ever heard him speak live, but I've been watching loads of DVDs of him recently. His teaching is deeply biblical, very accessible and hugely challenging. He has a wonderful ability to share his own failures, and yet speak with authority. When someone says something that I don't really want to hear, but they say it with a kind, genuine smile, I find it very hard not to listen.

Mike Pilavachi – as a speaker, he has many similar qualities to John Wimber. He communicates as a 'father', rather than as a teacher. His talks are spoken from the heart, they are said in love and they communicate real, relevant truth in an incredibly accessible way.

Timothy Keller – I only heard him speak for the first time a couple of months ago. His talks are full of grace, but also fresh insight. He speaks with great clarity and, again, a kindly authority.

How do you prepare your talks, and what is your starting point?

Different people prepare in different ways. The other day I went into a supermarket with Mike Pilavachi. He started to pick random ingredients off the shelves and put them in a trolley. I told him to stop – we needed to decide what we were going to cook before we bought any ingredients. He disagreed, and carried on just grabbing random items. It hit me later that he and I prepare talks in the same way we prepare meals.

When it comes to a meal, I'll decide what I'm going to cook, then I'll get the ingredients. With a talk, I'll decide on the topic, e.g. prayer, and then do the reading and research around that to pull together the content. Mike's default with cooking is to go to the fridge and make something out of whatever he finds in there. With talks, rather than the more structured 'title' and then 'research' approach, he'll have things brewing inside him from talks he's heard, books he's read, etc., then when it's time for him to give a talk, often those things will shape into a particular message he's been stewing over for a while.

I think the best approach is a combination of the two. I think it's always better to be thinking about what it is that God's been speaking to us about recently, and what he's been burdening our hearts with. When we have that sense we dig deeper, and research and think through the issue.

Often it might be the case that people are given a particular passage of Scripture to speak on (rather than getting to choose a topic and look for an issue being addressed within the Bible). If this is the case, then the passage has to be the starting point. Meditating on it, exploring it and trying to suss out what the main and the plain truths of the text are is the first step. We don't always have to find something radically new about a passage; usually our job is to communicate the same truth in a different light.

The other thing I've learned (the hard way) with talk preparation is that it's really easy to lose sight of the big picture. Often when I spend days thinking about and preparing a talk, by the time I'm on day three, the big, simple point I want to communicate is lost under a whole pile of information I've accumulated. Now, when I prepare a talk, I try to take a step back every forty-five minutes or so, and remind myself in a couple of lines what it is I want to say.

What would you say is the most important element of a talk?

The message we want people to leave with. It's a bit like a pen – the point of a pen is its point. The point of a talk is the point. The rest of the talk is just what we use to write this message on people's hearts. What this means is, when preparing a talk we've got to hone it until it's streamlined towards what we want to say. I'm definitely not a fan of taking forty-five minutes to say something that can be said in twenty-five (although I am a culprit). If our second or third point is not saying something new, or the same thing in a new way, we need to learn to leave it out. Communication is not about how long or short it is, or how funny or clever it is, the idea is to get the point across. All the other elements are hugely important – just saying something clearly doesn't mean someone will get the point. Humour, illustrations, fresh insights are all necessary, it's just remembering they are the means and not the end.

What would you say makes a good talk, good and a bad talk, bad?

Different preachers face different risks when it comes to 'bad' talks. Some are naturally heavy on content and light on illustration. Others are weak on content, but strong on illustration. It's being aware of your weaker areas and finding a way to work on them. Personally, I've struggled with a lack of clarity – it makes sense in my head, but somehow when it comes out, no one else understands it (that's my fault). I also have to battle to make sure what I'm saying is as exciting to my listeners as it is to me.

As far as 'good' talks go, the best preacher is the invisible preacher. Often we can think that if people leave saying 'what a great preacher' then we're doing well. The true test is when people leave thinking about what you've said; and even further, that they live out what you've said. A good talk is one that brings revelation to people's minds and hearts, and change to their lives. Ask yourself: how will people live differently having heard what I'm about to tell them?

Is there a particular verse or subject you love to speak on again and again?

Loving the Church is something that I'm committed to trying to do for the rest of my life. I'm not very good at it, but I'm learning. This is a message that I know lives in me – I'll be saying it for as long as anyone will listen.

Do you have any top tips for engaging an audience?

Be authentic. I think people can detect when someone is being honest, real and authentic. I also think people can see when someone is putting on a bit of a front. Great illustrations, creativity and not taking oneself too seriously are all really helpful, but they've got to go hand-in-hand with saying something and meaning it.

Andy studied theology at Cambridge University before joining Soul Survivor as the associate director in 2009. He is a speaker and author, and also heads up Soul61, the Soul Survivor discipleship course for emerging leaders.

6.

Hold it Together – Structure

Once all the great biblical material is prepared, it's time to think about structure. To understand the importance of good structure, think of a body: it is the skeleton that holds the many different parts together. For a talk, the structure helps our audience follow us, feel secure, stay with us, understand where we're going and remember what we've said. For some speakers, deciding on a structure can be a really tough part of preparation, one that induces fear or confusion. The key to structuring a talk is to order our material in such a way that it flows smoothly and logically. There isn't one way of doing this, but here are some suggestions:

- Tell people what you're going to say, say it, and then summarize what you've just said.
- Ask questions. For example, 'How?', 'Why?', 'When?' and 'What?' Then answer them one at a time.
- Let the passage dictate the structure by going through it line by line. So, for example, Isaiah 26:8 says 'Yes, LORD, walking in the way of your laws, we wait for you; your name and renown are the desire of our hearts.' I once heard a great talk where the speaker led us through the passage bit by bit, unpacking:

- *Yes*
- *Lord*
- *Walking*
- *In the way of your laws*
- *We wait for you*
- *Your name*
- *And renown*
- *Are the desire of our hearts*

It flowed smoothly and was logical because it followed the existing structure of the passage. This was simple and really effective.

- If you are speaking on a longer Bible passage, following the order of the words would also work. For example, if you are looking at the Parable of the Sower, having read the passage from Matthew 13 or Luke 8, and set the context, you could then unpack the meaning of the seed on the path, the seed on the rocky places, the seed among the thorns and then the seed on the good soil, before drawing out the main point of the whole parable.
- Use a solid illustration to provide the shape of the talk. I heard an example of this recently where the young guy giving the talk started by sharing a story about being invited to a wedding. His mum made sure he had a suit and had bought a gift. When the day came he had high hopes for what type of food might be served; later that day his hopes were dashed, but then it occurred to him that he wasn't the focus of the day, his friends getting married were. Having told this story in a very fun and funny way, he then returned to his story stage by stage, to talk about our sung corporate worship: the right clothes reflected preparing ourselves for worship; bringing a gift talked of the fact that each person should come ready to participate; the food not being his choice spoke of how worship isn't for us, it's

for God and that he is the focus of the celebration, it is for him and to him.

In this example the main illustration also provided the structure for the talk and it worked very well.

♦ Keep coming back to one question or statement, and repeat it before you illustrate it or unpack it. Then repeat it again before you talk about it from another angle.

However you choose to structure a talk, the important thing is that there must be some sense of a beginning, middle and end, and that each section or aspect flows into the next.

Smooth and Logical

How you decide which elements of your talk belong where might depend on the way you do your preparation:

♦ If you like to brainstorm and work visually, then go back to the flower image: write your 'one thing' in the centre and put all the elements around the outside. Then number the petals in the order that you want to present them.
♦ If you are someone who prepares out loud or in conversation, keep talking it through until you find the order that most makes sense.
♦ If you write your talks in full then you have the luxury of 'cut' and 'paste'. You can keep rearranging your material until you find the order that works.

In any case, we need to keep asking ourselves which sections belong naturally and logically together, and which bits of information must come sooner rather than later: What do I need to say now, so that I can say x further on? Is there a point I need to build up to? Is there an order of importance? Thinking through these questions should help us to work out a structure.

Then, in order to ensure our talk flows smoothly, we need to think about how we're going to move from section to section in a way that will carry our listeners with us. We need to think through how we can join sections together using non-contrived linking statements or paragraph-transitioning sentences. If we do this our listeners will be able to understand and follow where we're going.

Similarly, we should try to identify flags we can stake in the ground of our talk that let people know 'You are here'. A good flag might be a repetitive statement, or repetition of what we've just said before outlining the next thing we're going to say. This helps people stay with us and understand how what we're saying fits in to the overall picture. And if by any chance we've lost them, or their mind has wandered off to ponder their lunch options, then links, transitions and 'flags' will enable them get back on the same page as us so we can all journey on together.

The Structure for *O Come Let Us Adore Him*

The 'Flags'

The 'flags' in *O Come Let Us Adore Him* reminded the audience of what we had just looked at in the Bible before moving on to the next bit of the story. The structure of the story itself helped people to know where they were. Then in the second half, I kept the points short and always summarized them before moving on to the next one.

The Detailed Structure

- Intro
  - *My procrastination in preparing this talk*
  - *Busyness in run-up to Christmas*
  - *Time together to look at the story again*
- Shepherds
  - *Not the brightest of people*
  - *God chose them*
  - *Reaction – they went*
  - *God uses them to tell others*
- Magi
  - *Who they were*
  - *Background to King Herod and his reaction*
  - *Magi keep going till they reach Jesus*
  - *Brought their gifts*
  - *They obeyed*
- Delight and Duty
- Gifts and empty-handed
- Saviour and King
- Worship led to a response
- End – whether we are more like the shepherds or more like the Magi, let's worship Jesus.

Finally, structure is something that – as with most aspects of talk preparation – becomes easier and more natural over time. The good news is, you will soon find you do it without thinking.

Pause:

The next time you are listening to a talk, consider the structure. Is there an obvious one? Were you able to stay with the speaker as they led you through the material in a smooth and logical way? If so, what tools did they use to do this? And if not, what could they have done differently?

7.

Start on the Right Foot – Introducing Your Talk

How we begin a talk is really, really important. If we don't work hard on our introductions then much of the rest of our preparation might be wasted because no one is listening. It would be a bit like going on a long-awaited road trip with your best friend and realizing halfway up the M1 that you've left them behind. It's in our introductions that we gather people and bring a focus, so that everyone can then journey together for the rest of the talk. We need to think carefully about how to do this: how to create family and community; how to help people relax and engage with us; how to get them on board so that they actually listen to what we're saying.

Throughout our talks we want people to hear and receive our message, the truth of God's Word and to help them apply it to their own lives. It's worth thinking through, when writing your introduction, whether there's a way you can raise a hunger in the listener to receive truth, to hear what the Lord has to say, and to understand why they need this truth in their own lives. Ask yourself, 'How can I get the audience to the place where they feel they must listen to the rest of the talk? And how can I encourage them to listen to me?' If we can get them at the beginning, we stand more of a chance of keeping them throughout the talk. If we lose them at the start, we've probably lost them throughout.

The introduction is our opportunity to give the audience someone they can relate to. If they feel like they can connect with us, then they are much more likely to listen to us, if they listen to us they are more likely to put into action what we're teaching. Telling a funny story about ourselves, for example, is not necessarily self-indulgent or egotistical, but instead can be a really important part of the process. Previous generations, or some churches with a more traditional speaking style, may disagree with this. They might want a speaker to be invisible and just preach the Word. But this generation wants to hear truth from people, real people.

We were made for relationship and contact with each other, and that also has to be true in our preaching. The introduction to our talk is the perfect opportunity to not only lay out where we want to go, but also to introduce ourselves as a real flesh-and-blood person.

So what can we do to ensure that we start strong and grab people's attention, helping them to connect, not only to the importance of our message, but also with ourselves, the bringer of the message? Here are some ideas and examples:

- A great place to start is to look and sound confident, calm, and happy to be there. If you are none of these things, fake it! It really will help people relax and get ready to receive what you're about to say. Looking and sounding confident and relaxed is easier when you sense you have a word from God for the group of people you're about to address, then no matter how inadequate you feel there is a sense of purpose and anticipation – sometimes even excitement.
- Don't tell your audience that you're nervous, as they could get more caught up in worrying about whether or not you'll make it through the next twenty minutes, than in

hearing and receiving your message. Take a deep breath before you get up to speak, and then smile.

- It's good to introduce yourself, but the amount of detail you go into will depend on how well you're known in that context, on whether this is your first time in front of a certain group or if you see the same faces – and they see yours – every week. Don't forget that even if you stand up to speak every Sunday there will often be visitors present. If you had a group of people over for pizza, and in the midst of that group there was someone you had never met before, you wouldn't ignore them, but as part of making them feel comfortable you'd make sure you introduced yourself. This lets them know that they are welcome. In the same way, if you're speaking to a known crowd, for the sake of any guests on that day, it's nice for them to at least know your name.

- It is helpful to assume that the audience is not that interested. As pessimistic as that sounds, it will certainly be true for at least one person there. Even those who are interested can be easily distracted, tired, feeling unwell or uncomfortable. You have to get them to a place where they want to listen to you and your message. At the very start, you need to get them on board, wake them up if necessary, and start to capture their attention and imagination. Think about learning your first sentence by heart so you can start strong.

- Introductions are also really important in setting the scene for where you're going to be taking people. This doesn't have to be by outlining your structure for them (though it could be), but at least give them an idea of what you want to talk about. If you're going to plot where you're going make sure you do this clearly. Keep it nice and simple, without too much detail.

If we're speaking on a topic that is based in part on our own testimony then it's great to start with this. Beginning with our story will capture people's attention, get them interested and help them be more receptive to the teaching we go on to give as we unpack that testimony. For example, many years ago I suffered with depression. Whenever I speak on this subject I always start with my story so that people know I understand what they are going through, that I have a reason to speak, and a reason to give hope because I've been where they have been. Similarly, when I asked a friend, who has come through an eating disorder, to teach on that subject I asked her to start with her own powerful story of struggle and healing. Another friend of mine is an excellent communicator, especially in the area of sexual purity. When she speaks on this subject, I always encourage her to start with her own honest testimony of struggle and mistakes in the past, and how the Lord has forgiven, redeemed and healed her. Apart from anything else there are so many barriers that people put up to hearing truth on painful or difficult subjects, and sharing your own testimony early on can knock these barriers down.

Introduction to *O Come Let Us Adore Him*

I started the talk by describing the difficulty I had preparing it, the obstacles I encountered, and then my procrastination. This led up to how busy Christmas is and how it is easy to lose sight of the Christmas story, which got me to the place where I could say, 'So let's take time looking at it tonight.' In hindsight, I would keep some of the humour but clean it up and shorten it so there was a little less preamble.

Ideas for Introductions

- Strong illustration
- Personal testimony
- Raise the questions your talk is going to answer
- Outline what you are going to cover
- Use trivia or statistics on the topic you're speaking on
- Tell a humorous story

We want to go in strong, with a good, clear, confident opening that will hook people into the journey from the word go. And then, as with any other section of a talk, we need to think about how we transition from our 'introductions' into the main body of what we want to say as smoothly as possible.

Pause:

Think about the last time you spoke. In your preparation, did you pay enough attention to the beginning of your talk? How did you begin, how did you encourage people to get on board? If not, what could you do differently next time? Also, in the coming weeks, pay attention to how other speakers kick off their talks – what do you find effective, welcoming, clear and real? What has been less effective?

Interview

Beth Redman

Beth is a simple, yet never simplistic speaker. She will often speak on one thing – one verse, one line, one thought – and illuminate it from many different angles, with honesty, intimacy, passion and self-disclosure. There is something about her style of communication that allows the Holy Spirit to open up the audience to God – it's totally disarming and engaging.

Why do we preach? What do you understand the purpose of preaching to be?

We preach because we are called to be evangelists and to tell others the good news about Jesus. We preach also to encourage and comfort the Church, and to bring deeper understanding of who God is. Preaching is not a rant or a legalistic telling off. In the dictionary, the word 'preach' means to proclaim and to earnestly give religious or moral advice in a persistent way.

It's a bit like this: 'Here is what I have seen, here is what I've experienced and know to be true; here is what I've dug deep to understand about Jesus.'

Fuelled by that passion for Jesus and with a sincere love for his people, a preacher desires to earnestly teach and encourage others to know, love and obey God.

Have you always wanted to speak? When did you know it was part of your calling?

I feel like I am an evangelist first and foremost, but I am also passionate about encouraging and teaching the Church, and in particular encouraging and teaching young women. I never imagined myself teaching, but one day, my pastor, Mike Pilavachi, just sort of asked/made me! I wasn't even sure how a speaker was supposed to prepare a talk, but I just opened up Psalm 103, which I had been reading at the time, and line by line, I tried to very simply encourage others with the amazing truth that was on the page.

It is such a beautiful psalm – full of truth, and both sobering and sharpening. It starts 'Praise the LORD, O my soul, and forget not all his benefits' [Psalm 103:2]. It is David's encouragement to himself to remember all that God has been so faithful to do. Remembering led David into a place of rejoicing. It was such a simple message and I was terrified beforehand, but at the end lots of people were prayed for and responded so beautifully to God. I was floored that God can use anyone or anything . . . even me, apparently!

Is there any part of talk preparation or delivery that you've particularly had to work on?

Teaching is a huge responsibility, and I think it requires a mature discipline to both prepare conscientiously, and to have a humble open ear or heart to hear what God wants to say. I have definitely had to work on a real dread of preaching. I started to make it about me (yuck!) and I needed to get my ears and eyes off myself and back onto what God was wanting to say to others. If you make it about you, or worry about what people think, you shouldn't be teaching.

Who has inspired you as a speaker in the past, and who do you like to listen to now?

I particularly love listening to women speak. Right now I love Joyce Meyer; she has studied the Bible, and her love and knowledge of Jesus is truly infectious. She is also very down to earth and self-deprecating, which is hilarious to listen to. With Joyce, all at once you are laughing, learning and getting your spiritual butt kicked.

How do you prepare talks, and what is your starting point?

I take something God has put on my heart – a verse, a story or an experience – and I try to simply, with just one or two points, teach it to others.

What would you say is the most important element of a talk?

Being accessible by keeping it simple. I would have to say I believe the most important element of a talk, from a technical point of view, is being able to sum up what your message is about in one point. People need to come away and say this one thing is what that message was about, and this is what I need to do, and this is what I have learned today.

What would you say makes a good talk, good and a bad talk, bad?

A good talk is totally Christ-centred and easy to follow. A bad talk is one that has not been prepared properly, is too much about the person, or has too many random, rambling points. I have given both varieties.

Can you think of any mistakes you've made, or problems you've had to overcome?

I would say the dread of giving a talk has caused me to make terrible mistakes. There have been occasions when I have got so caught up with nerves that it has distracted my preparation and my delivery. I think the more you love God and are secure in him, the easier it is to be used by him and be a blessing to others. As a teacher, I need to keep my eyes on the real issue, which is my amazing God – it's all about him, at all times, and all for his glory, and not, not, not about me.

Is there a particular verse or subject you love to speak on again and again?

Hebrews 12:1–3. It is so easy to preach from this passage because it fires me up and has gripped my heart so much over the years. Hebrews 12 speaks so plainly, simply and wonderfully about Jesus, and why we are here and how we are to live. I could speak about this passage forever and not get bored; it is so powerful and makes me fired up just thinking about it.

Do you have any top tips for engaging an audience?

Keep it simple and succinct. And master the art of being completely yourself, while keeping your eyes on Jesus throughout. It captivates others and most importantly glorifies God.

It says in 2 Corinthians 5:14, 'For Christ's love compels us'. That is the place and the passion from which we are ultimately speaking; longing to love and honour him at all times, and to be desperate that others know and love him fully too.

Beth is an author, speaker and Dove Award-winning songwriter. She is married to the worship leader and songwriter, Matt Redman, and they have five children. Beth is the UK director of A21, an organization committed to abolishing twenty-first-century slavery, particularly in trafficking. Beth loves her life, her friends, laughing, and most of all, Jesus.

8

Bringing Life to Truth – Illustrations

Recently, I was listening to a theological lecture on the culture into which the Christian faith was born. I loved it! Having not been in that kind of learning environment for a while I can't pretend that my poor brain wasn't being stretched, but the speaker was excellent, communicating with gracious intelligence and clarity on her given subject. Everyone was listening attentively, scribbling away in books, tapping away on laptops. And then about an hour into the lecture, the speaker shared a story from her own life to illustrate a particular point. Suddenly and tangibly, the atmosphere in the room changed, as did the corporate body language of her audience. We sat up, leant forward. We had been interested before, but now she really had us.

The speaker had no need to win me over. I wanted to be there – more than that, I had paid to be there, as had the others who were in the room. We were already sold on the subject and had a purpose in listening. The illustration wasn't earth-shatteringly brilliant or intriguingly personal, but even in that environment it added life and caught our attention.

Now imagine a typical Sunday service in the church you attend, and perhaps even speak in. Many come to the service distracted and sometimes disengaged. They haven't a clue what the speaker is going to speak on and why they need to hear it. They might not want to listen to what he or she has to say, or they might find it hard because of other things on their mind (children needing their attention, or distractions about the week ahead). So, as speakers, we have to help them engage. In the previous chapter, we looked at how important it is to connect the audience with us personally, as well as with our message directly (in fact, the former could well lead to the latter). One of the best ways to do this is using good illustrations: a story, an example, or a comparison from our life, or the lives of others, that gives the point colour, explains it or clarifies it.

I believe that illustrations are absolutely essential in communicating with today's audience. I've yet to see an audience that doesn't come alive or connect in a new way when a story is told. Illustrations are what make a talk interesting, colourful, real and funny – they help our audience relate to our material, and they hold their attention like little else.

We might use illustrations that are factual, directly showing what the teaching looks like in real life – times when we or others have done, or not done, the very thing we're talking about. Or we might use indirect illustrations – stories or analogies that explain a point in a less obvious, often fun way.

Direct Illustrations

These types of illustrations come from our own lives, or someone else's. The internet is a good sourcing ground for this type of illustration, as are our friends and family, and Christian biographies. So, for instance, if we were talking about God as our provider, we might share a testimony of where God has provided for us in a wonderful and obvious way. Here are a couple of other examples.

I once spoke on the subject of taking every thought captive

and making it obedient to Christ, in regard to the importance of repentance and rejection of lies. I shared from my own life a time when God – through the wisdom of trusted friends – called me to identify, and then write a list, of the lies I'd been believing. Then opposite these lies I wrote down God's truth. This was a practical illustration of what it means to take certain thoughts captive and make them obedient to Christ.

Another time, I talked on the subject of the reconciling work of the Cross. To reconcile is to put right, resolve, bring together – this is what the word literally means, but I didn't want it to be left as a concept. On the internet, I came across a story of a charity in South Africa that had been started up by a mother of a murdered daughter and the man who had issued the directive to kill her child. This unlikely pair were now working together to see peace in South Africa. They were reconciled – somehow, unimaginably and miraculously, these two people came together.

Illustrations like these mean that we show we aren't just spouting good theory and nice ideas from the Bible. We can show examples of what that truth actually looks like in real life. It puts a face to the teaching, and helps unpack it further, making it real. In the interview with Mary Pytches, later on in this book, she points out that she consistently finds that using real-life examples opens people's eyes to the issues in their own lives, even more than the careful teaching and theory. We need to pray for good illustrations for our talks that will help bring a teaching point to life.

These sorts of illustrations also double up as application (more on this in the chapter on application) because they are not only giving clarity to the point, and showing what it looks like, but they also give people ideas as to how they might live that truth out.

When using this kind of illustration, we must make sure they aren't all too big, too 'out there'. Stories of super-Christians who have seen people raised from the dead or evangelized a nation are great at lifting our faith, but if we hear too many of these, we'll all feel like failures. We need to keep coming back to everyday illustrations that work in everyday life for the everyday person. We must also make sure that not every illustration is about us, especially not a perceived celebration of how great we are, or how fantastically we've done something. On the other hand, we shouldn't litter a talk with lots of examples of how awful we are. We should be real and humble. Illustrations are meant to bring life to a point, not distract from it. It's great to be real, but we do this to remove barriers, not lower the bar. It's helpful to remind people that we're all the same, facing the same struggles, but it's not helpful to give permission to sin.

If we're going to be sharing a personal and perhaps painful story, we need to think how to help the audience relax and receive what we're saying. We don't want them to get caught up in feeling so sorry for us that they're distracted from the point we're trying to make. One way of doing this is by letting them know we're fine, that this story is in the past and doesn't hurt anymore. Another way is with a bit of gentle humour. Recently, I heard someone speak who was using a story from her own life about her dad's premature death. Just as I was starting to feel dreadful for her, she threw in a very light, appropriate joke that showed all of us she really was OK, even though the circumstances were painful. The use of humour can be a tough one to pull off. We don't want to come across as harsh or unfeeling, but we do need to think through how we prevent our listeners from getting hung up on the wrong thing.

Similarly, when sharing from our own life we should check in advance that we are ready to put that information out there. Once we've shared something publicly we can't take it back. We need to think about how we will feel if others who have gone through something similar then want to talk to us about our experience. Is the story still too fresh – and therefore too painful – to share? Has the situation or at least the feeling been resolved (if not, talking about it publicly could feel like pulling a plaster off a healing wound)? Will telling that story affect friends of family members who will hear it? We shouldn't share a personal story without thinking through the implications for ourselves and others.

Indirect Illustrations

The other way of using illustrations in a talk is the more light-hearted way, where we tell a story that has meaning – subtle or obvious – to explain our point. I'm a big fan of this style, where I tell a slightly tenuous story that doesn't initially seem to have anything to do with what I'm saying. However, on closer examination, or as the point is drawn out, the audience (hopefully) begins to see the meaning. Here are a couple of examples.

In the talk I referred to earlier about taking thoughts captive, I started by telling a story about being bitten as a child by a gerbil that had escaped its cage. It held on to me with its teeth (very painful) so I shook it off, to then have to go through the rigmarole of recapturing it. I pointed out that what I should have done was hold on to it long enough to put it back in its cage, even though two sharp teeth were painfully puncturing my finger. The aim of my story was to show that sometimes we have to 'hold on' to painful thoughts long enough to deal with them and bring them to Jesus.

Another time, I told the story of how when I was very young I answered the phone to a lady who attended the church where my dad was the pastor. She wanted to speak to him, but I told her that he couldn't come to the phone because he was in the bath. So she asked to speak to Mum instead, but I told her she was in the bath too. When Mum and Dad became available and I passed the message on, they were of course a little embarrassed. They explained away the shared bath through some tall story about water shortages, and trained me in the art of evasive message taking. I used this story, having gained permission from my parents, to illustrate a point on passing on information.

Disguise and Don't Distract

If you're sharing a story about someone else, make sure you've asked their permission, and if necessary, disguised them sufficiently. Also be wary of using stories that will get people's attention for the wrong reasons, i.e. if you hint at something that leaves them guessing, or if there is a suggestion of gossip or scandal. People are naturally nosey and this could leave them more hung up on the unanswered questions than the point itself. If the story doesn't work, better to leave it out than to hint and tell half a story.

Stories can work well because they stick in people's minds, and if we can make them laugh, all the better. They might be long stories, or a couple of lines. It doesn't matter as long as they serve the purpose of our talk. Try to use stories that people can relate to. This is what the best comedians do – Michael McIntyre is so funny because he makes everyday observations about life that we all experience and can connect to. However. illustrations don't have to be funny. Jesus' teaching style was to tell stories that everyone could relate to, using the language and culture of the day.

Telling Stories

All speakers need to learn how to tell stories well so they contain just the right amount of detail and aren't too drawn out. Some people find it difficult to leave anything out, particularly when telling an important story or testimony from their own lives – this can make stories very long and messy:

- Bear in mind, right from the beginning, what the point is of you sharing a particular story. With that firmly in mind, it will act as a guide to what detail you should include and what can be left out.
- There needs to be enough detail to paint the picture, but try to avoid unnecessary information that will clutter up the story and potentially confuse your listeners.
- Know your facts in advance. Avoid: 'It was on a Thursday afternoon, at about 3 o'clock. No, maybe 4 o'clock. Actually it was Friday. Anyway, it was sometime in an afternoon last week. . .'
- Try writing out your own testimony (either how you came to know Jesus or a significant story in your life) in the light of these tips.
- Practise your story on someone – they will find it easier than you to spot the unnecessary detail.

This type of illustration is happening to us and our friends and family all the time, we just need to grab them and use them well. So start recording any story that makes you laugh or cry, or that makes you feel angry, scared or embarrassed. Any strong emotion will help your story be a memorable one. It's great to get into the habit of recording stories like these, even if to begin with we can't see how to use them. Having made a note of the stories, we can then chat to God about what they could illustrate.

Recently, I remembered something that happened to me several years ago. I was about to come to the end of my job at Soul Survivor (I thought for good at the time, but came back a year later). In my final week, my boss, Liz, said she needed me to take minutes for a meeting, and that lunch would be provided. Ever passionate about food, my inner fear was: how would I take minutes and eat at the same time? So en route to the meeting I stopped off at McDonalds for a Quarter-Pounder Meal. Thus satisfied, I headed to where I was meant to be, only to discover that it wasn't a meeting at all, but a surprise leaving party for me – complete with three-course dinner. I didn't have the heart to tell the clever chefs that I'd already eaten, so I spent the whole time picking at my food, pretending I was too overcome with emotion to eat.

As I remembered this incident, it struck me that it could make a good illustration for a talk, but I had no idea how I could use it. So I wrote it up and put it in my 'illustrations' folder and forgot about it for a while. Then a few months later, I was writing a talk about genealogies and long lists in the Bible, and how so many of us struggle with them, and are tempted to see them as a waste of time and skip over them. But I wanted to make the point that since 'all Scripture is God-breathed and useful' (see 2 Timothy 3:16) there must be something beneficial about them. As I was searching for an illustration for the talk, I remembered my leaving do. I used it to show I'd made a mistake in thinking there would be no sustenance for me in the meeting, so I looked for my food elsewhere. In the same way, we can mistakenly think there is no 'meat' in all the genealogies of the Bible, so we race past them, not realizing there is good stuff right there. And then I went on to talk about the good stuff to be found in and around the long lists of names and numbers we find throughout the Bible (e.g. what such lists say about God's people as a community rather than individuals).

I used to think that speakers seemed to have weird, funny or embarrassing things happen to them just because they were speakers. As if God, in trying to help them be more interesting, made weird, funny or embarrassing things happen to them. Now I realize we all have things happen to us, speakers just tell more people. So even if you're not too sure how you could use a particularly interesting, funny or embarrassing story, record it somewhere and you could well find it comes in handy.

Make a Note

Don't leave recording illustrations (or quotes, thoughts, talk ideas) to chance. Your memory will let you down, so keep a note on your phone, a document in your computer or a file in a drawer as things happen or come to mind.

If you can't find an illustration, try asking God to remind you of illustrations you can use to bring your point to life. I honestly find that whenever I do this he will bring something to mind – he seems to be up for helping me with this one. God's not just there to show us the deep theological stuff – I believe he wants to breathe his life into every part of our talks, so that the truth will be heard, remembered and received.

One way of using these kinds of illustrations is in our introduction. They work well because they serve to relax us and our audience, and help them feel connected to us.

Illustrations also begin to gently paint a picture of where we are heading in the rest of our talk.

Again, as with any aspect of our talk, if we're going to bring in an illustration, we shouldn't just throw it in with no explanation or unpacking. Draw out its meaning. This is especially important if we have taken a while to tell the illustration in the first place. If the illustration doesn't perfectly shed light on our point then we should tell the audience. We should show where the analogy falls down, so that at least people don't draw out the wrong meaning. We need to make sure the illustration is needed and useful to the talk, and if not, leave it out and save it for another day.

I sincerely believe that a talk must contain illustrations because it will be these stories and examples that bring the talk to life and hold people's attention. We can't fool ourselves that people will listen just because we're talking. We have to help engage them. People's attention span is short. Stories are essential to keeping up the interest level. Illustrations communicate something in a way that simply stating it can't do. Telling a story can often be the point when people 'get it' – suddenly there is clarity and understanding. I usually try to find one illustration for every main section or point of a talk.

A word of warning about illustrations (from my own experience and feedback I've received). It's easy to sound passionate and relaxed when telling stories, but we need to make sure we apply that same passion and energy to our core content, and when talking directly about the Bible. Also, we should ensure our illustrations are – like any other aspect – tailored to our audience. A group of teenagers probably won't want to hear a load of stories about DIY, marriage and babies (it took me a while to work that out).

Finally, beware of lies or exaggeration. The truth is always the best policy. I don't think we can lie just for the sake of a good illustration. If we are using a fictional tale, then say that. If someone found out our 'story' was just that – a story – they may start to question the truth of the rest of our message.

Illustrations in *O Come Let Us Adore Him*

- Opening story about struggling to prepare the talk.
- Painting pictures of who shepherds and Magi were in 'now' terms.
- Personal testimony about coming to God empty-handed.
- My mum's gift drawer (when talking about the shepherds coming empty-handed)
- The Barrier Reef – the 'wow' and 'whoa' of God.

Pause:

Think of an illustration – either a real example from your life or someone else's, or a story to draw out the meaning – for these three sermon ideas:

1. *Walking on water requires a step of faith.*
2. *The Lord is my shepherd, I shall not want.*
3. *The Church is one body made of many parts.*

Keeping It Real: Removing Barriers to Truth

One thing that really connects with people, particularly younger people, is honesty and vulnerability. Keeping it real communicates like little else. People don't want to hear the truth of God's Word via an invisible communicator, but from someone imperfect and human, just like them. God knew the impact of this when he sent his Son (human, though in his case, perfect) to live as one of us, to experience life as we experience it, to know what it is to suffer and face temptations. This is the power of the incarnation – Emmanuel, God with us. As speakers, we can't kid ourselves that people want any less than that from us. If Jesus, though perfect, could come and relate to humankind, we certainly can't think that we – with all our imperfections – can get away with hiding behind a pulpit or microphone, and presenting only the best of ourselves.

So we need to find places in our talks where we can share our own experience: the things that have worked for us and the things that didn't; the things we've struggled with and which, with God's help, we have overcome (or are in the process of overcoming).

Having said this, it doesn't mean that we share every sinful thought and deed to a room full of people. This may well not be helpful for them or us, and can be very distracting. I would say the rule of thumb is to take down barriers to truth without lowering the bar. So we're never saying sin is OK, but we are saying that we all struggle, we are all flesh and blood.

Quotes

A well-chosen quote can bring a great perspective on the point we're making, show what other people think about an issue, or bring a humorous take on the subject matter. Using quotes in our talk can add interest, value and impact and – as with other illustrations – can be a great way of unpacking a subject. Here are some ideas on how to use quotes well:

- Think about the relevance of a quote to the particular audience: a group of older people might not care what Bono has to say about anything, whereas many 20- or 30-somethings will relate to his take on a subject. The ideal is to find people who connect with the culture and the people.
- Use the internet to search for good quotes on a specific subject. The internet can also be helpful in clarifying a quote and ensuring it's accurate, rather than saying 'so and so once said something along the lines of' which doesn't carry much weight.
- If you're going to use a quote, then make sure it's not too long: if it's more than a paragraph, you could well lose people.
- If possible, have the quote put up on a screen so that people can see it – people are much more likely to remember something that they hear if they see it too.
- Don't use more than two to three quotes in a talk, otherwise it will feel cluttered and it will feel like there isn't enough of you in the talk.

As with anything, if we're going to use quotes, we need to use them well – draw out the point we're making by using that quote. We shouldn't just read it and leave people to guess or decipher why we included it. If we have to explain it too much, it's probably not a great quote to use.

Pause:

Who are the people that 'speak' to your generation or to your main audience? Who do they relate to and respect?

9.

More Than Words – Visuals and Multimedia

Another practical aspect of presenting a good talk is the use of multimedia – PowerPoint, DVD or YouTube clips, songs, lighting, dance and drama. This is not my area of expertise; creativity doesn't come naturally to me, and the times I've seen multimedia used well in a talk by someone else are few and far between. But this doesn't mean we shouldn't consider it, because the few times I have seen it done well, it has been very effective in making a talk memorable and interesting. A really great PowerPoint presentation, for example, can reinforce a message and provide a strong focus. If you've ever heard Mark Greene, Executive Director of The London Institute of Contemporary Christianity, speak, you will know what I mean. Mark is from an advertising background and uses images to illustrate the point he is making. It is always so simple and so cleverly done. The few times I have attempted a (very amateur) slideshow, I've been amazed at the feedback I've received in terms of how helpful it is for people, especially from those who are more stimulated by what they see than by what they hear.

If you are going to use multimedia in a talk, here are some practical things we should think through:

* Check in advance that the right facilities are available and working, and that the quality of what you've prepared is suitable for showing.
* With this in mind, you will need to arrive at the venue early enough to test everything is working as it should be, and either have a back-up prepared, or know how you will manage without it if you have to.
* When using passages from the Bible, or any additional written content – such as a quote – it is good to give people a visual reference by putting it up on the screen.
* When displaying words on a screen, you need to ensure the words are big enough to be seen right at the back, and in every corner of the room. Check with the technical person what that means for the setting you're in. (It's usually point size 44 or above.)
* Think through your colour scheme. Yellow words on a pink background will not only look pretty offensive, but will be hard to read. A safer and clearer colour scheme would be white words on a blue or black background.
* Don't put a transcript of your talk or too much information on the screen. Use key words or phrases that highlight or summarize what you are saying. If your audience can read your talk, why would they need to listen to you? If you put too much information in front of them they will stop looking at you, and the connection you've been building could be lost.
* Using strong images that add to what you're saying and that layer your communication can be even better than using words.
* If you want to use a DVD clip, think about burning a copy that fades in and out to the exact part you want to show. Not only will this look very slick, but it will prevent that

awkward fumbling that can so often happen at the end of a desired clip, where the speaker wants to move on but the technical support is still catching up.

- Also think about the appropriateness of the clip to the audience and the setting. We recently had an example at church where the particular clip contained a brush with near-nudity, and some rather interesting words, which, with a bit of know-how, could have been fuzzed or bleeped out.

- As with other types of illustrations, if a piece of multimedia needs a ten-minute explanation before it makes sense to your audience, then it's probably not worth using. Think carefully about the length in advance, and ask yourself whether the amount of time spent focusing on the explanation justifies using it.

- If you are planning on using anything too out of the ordinary, make sure you check in advance with the person responsible for the whole service. Most people would appreciate some advance warning and the opportunity to raise any objections.

If we're going to use multimedia, let's do it well or not at all, and let's only use it if it serves our talk – not just to entertain or because we think it's what speakers should do these days. Let's consider this as one way of helping our talks come to life but, in my opinion, there are other things that are more essential, for example, real illustrations.

Finally, if using multimedia is something that really appeals to you, don't forget the need to keep the audience connected with you as a speaker. Remember the importance of eye contact in helping people stay attentive. If there are too many visuals in front of your listeners, it might be hard to keep in tune with you and the message.

Pause:

Remember that if this technical stuff doesn't come naturally to you, it may do to someone you know, or someone in your church. So why not ask them to get involved? Is there anyone you can ask to help you do something, from researching images on the internet to coming up with and implementing creative concepts?

Interview

Pete Hughes

When I was relatively new to this speaking thing, I had the privilege of working with Pete and would so often run talks or thoughts past him. I still, several years on, miss his input. Pete is a very rich speaker: thorough in his approach to God's Word, dedicated to its outworking in our everyday lives, and very, very funny. He has an understated authority and wisdom, and is incredibly easy to listen to.

Why do we preach? What do you understand the purpose of preaching to be?

I believe we preach to communicate God's truth and to inspire movement. I don't mean we preach to move people in the emotional sense, I mean we preach towards change. By placing Christ at the front and centre, and by providing people with a vision of God's kingdom, we seek to move people to do something with the hope that they begin to align their lives, values and actions with that of Christ's. Good preaching always bears fruit in changed lives.

Have you always wanted to speak? When did you know it was part of your calling?

I only really knew that preaching was something I wanted to do more of when I started doing it. I recently read a great quote on the subject of calling by Howard Thurman, who said: 'Don't ask yourself what the world needs. Ask yourself what makes you come alive and then go do that. Because what the world needs is people who have come alive.'[5] I guess I feel like part of me comes alive when I preach, and I think it's because it's something I feel God has called me to.

Can you remember the first talk you ever gave? If so, how did it go?

The first proper talk I gave was at a church in South Africa. I still have the notes. It was a pretty dreadful talk, but it was the best I could do at the time. I've done plenty of worse talks since!

Is there any part of talk preparation or delivery that you've particularly had to work on?

I've worked hard at becoming a better story-teller as I think good story-telling is critical to good preaching. I think the Word becomes flesh in great preaching, so I've also worked hard at trying to give more of myself away in preaching. By that, I mean I try to demonstrate how I'm seeking (and normally struggling) to embody what I'm saying in my day-to-day life.

Who has inspired you as a speaker in the past, and who do you like to listen to now?

The people who have inspired me most as a preacher include Mike Pilavachi, Louie Giglio, Don Williams, Mary Pytches, Rich Nathan, Rob Bell, my dad and many more. They're all very different in style, but are brilliant at bringing the Scriptures to life. They're also fantastic at engaging with people's hearts as well as minds.

How do you prepare your talks, and what is your starting point?

It depends really on what type of talk I am giving. If I'm asked to speak on a passage from Scripture, I'll start by reading a few commentaries on the passage. In other words, I normally first work on the content until I think I have something valuable to say. I think a good marker of having great content is that if you write up the talk as an article, it's worth reading. You'll then know that you're not leaning too heavily on engagement. (And by the way, I've heard many talks in which the preacher has engaged the audience brilliantly, but has had nothing really to say.) When I have the content and a rough structure in place, I try to bring the content to life with stories, quotes, humour and examples of how I'm trying to embody the message in my own life. I quite like the image of God breathing life into the dry bones (Ezek. 37). Applying this to preaching (I have the feeling this may be slightly heretical!) I see the content and structure like the bones that need to come to life through the preacher and the use of stories and humour. And obviously – and far more importantly –

we believe the Spirit brings the truth of Scripture to life in and through the preacher.

What would you say is the most important element of a talk?

Preaching is not entertainment. That doesn't mean that great preaching isn't entertaining. Instead it means that the main purpose of preaching is to communicate God's heart and truth to his people. I therefore think that having something valuable to say (i.e. revelation from God) is the critical ingredient that distinguishes preaching from stand-up comedy or other forms of communication.

What would you say makes a good talk, good and a bad talk, bad?

In my mind a good talk needs to hold a healthy tension between content and engagement. Forgettable talks either tend towards great content and dreadful engagement, or dreadful content and great engagement. We normally remember the ones with dreadful content and dreadful engagement (because they were that bad), and always remember the ones with great content and great engagement. This is the tension I'm aiming for: I don't always get it right, but it's what I always work towards.

Can you think of any particular mistakes you've made, or problems you've had to overcome?

The greatest mistake I've ever made in preaching is to allow my sense of identity to get caught up in it. When you start preaching in order to win people's love and affection, you know you're in trouble. When you preach well you feel great, and when you preach badly you feel like a failure. And although some of that is natural (we all want to do well), it can get to the place where preaching becomes more about you than about building up others. The best preachers preach from a place of already knowing that they're loved – they don't need a great talk to prove it. Only then are you truly free to preach what God places on your heart.

Is there a particular verse or subject you love to speak on again and again?

I love preaching about God's love. I never get bored of it!

Do you have any top tips for engaging an audience?

Firstly, become a great story-teller. People are always drawn to stories. They provide a great way of bringing truth to life, and speak to the heart as well as the mind.

Secondly, become a vulnerable communicator. People hunger for authenticity. In a post-modern context, where people value authenticity above abstract truth, people aren't always asking is it true – they're asking is it real and does it make a difference to my life. This means that sharing something of yourself is critical. Also, truth is best received in the context of relationship. Therefore, in my opinion, all great preaching is relational. It isn't purely about imparting information, but is also about connecting and relating with the congregation.

Thirdly, become a passionate student of Scripture. Passion is contagious. I personally love studying theology, and find that it keeps my passion for God's Word alive. It has also provided some great tools with which to engage with the Bible at a deeper level (and there are some great books out there to help you do this, e.g. Gordon Fee's *How to Read the Bible for All It's Worth* [Zondervan 2003]). If you're in it for the long haul, I think every preacher needs to become a student of theology. That doesn't necessarily mean formal study, but it does mean beginning to read books that will help you plumb the depths of Scripture.

Pete is married to Bee, and together they lead King's Cross Church (KXC), a recent Anglican church plant into the King's Cross area of London. Pete previously worked at Soul Survivor before joining the leadership team St Mary's, Bryanston Square in London.

10

Beating the Jargon Factor – Using Inclusive Language

I once heard a talk by a guy who was way more intelligent than I am, speaking on a subject that was completely new to me and – if I'm honest – slightly over my head. Throughout the talk the speaker repeatedly used the phrase, 'as we all know', but actually, I didn't know. Did every one else? I asked a few people later and found out that, thankfully, I wasn't the only dunce in the class. Long before hearing this particular talk, I've had the personal rule to never use the phrase 'as we all know' and have strongly discouraged others from using it too. The reason for this is that we all want to feel included and those four words draw a line in the sand: are you in or are you out? We want to feel part of the gang, not on the outside of some exclusive club. When it comes to giving a talk, we need to find ways to ensure our language includes everybody and that we don't unthinkingly exclude anyone in our audience. Here are some tips as to how you can best avoid doing this:

- Try to ensure you're addressing 'us' and 'we' not 'you'. As a speaker you are not more holy and anointed or sorted than the next person – you just happen to be the one standing on a stage doing the talking. So preaching is not us at them – telling people what they should be doing and thinking – but instead journeying and learning together.

- If you've been a Christian for a long time, you need to be especially aware that your natural language is the language of the Church, which isn't the language of a 'normal' person. This doesn't mean that you stay away from key words of our faith such as redeem, save, righteous, justify, etc. These are important (and biblical) words, but you might need a line or two to define them.

- We might not tend to use phrases like 'blood of the lamb' anymore, but we still use Christian jargon – phrases that don't mean much to those outside of our Christian club: 'on my heart' (I've been thinking and pondering), 'check in my spirit' (that didn't feel right), 'quiet times' (time spent talking to and worshipping God alone, which shouldn't necessarily be quiet at all). This kind of thing should be avoided, or at the very least explained.

- Similarly, you should try to avoid referring to events or organizations that only committed members of the church would be aware of. The same would be true for 'famous' Christians such as John Wimber or Brother Andrew. Again, it doesn't mean you have to avoid referring to these altogether, but a (very) brief explanation will ensure people know you are welcoming them into the 'conversation'.

- Someone else will spot your use of jargon and exclusive language much quicker than you will. So this is one of the reasons why it's good to have someone else go through your talk in advance and critique it afterwards.

- And, my golden rule, never say 'as we all know'

Whenever we speak, let's do all we can to make our talks as accessible as possible for the entire audience.

Pause:

Over the next few weeks, listen out when people are speaking, and review your own talks to see if you can spot 'Christianese' or exclusive language. Consciously think through a more suitable alternative.

11.

Bringing Truth to Life – Application

Have you ever walked out of a talk thinking, that was great, but who cares? If so, chances are the speaker didn't give any time or thought to apply the truth of their message to the real and concrete stuff of your everyday life.

Application is a key part of any talk. The 'how' and 'what now' always needs to be covered. As J.John, evangelist and communicator, says, 'Exhortation without application leads to frustration.' If we set standards without helping people get there, it's just a heavy burden to carry or empty knowledge with no relevance to real life. Without application, a talk is a great Bible study at best or a collection of ideas at worst. Without application, a talk can be defeating. Our talks should be more than nice, interesting, fun, engaging and godly theory, so we need to give time to drawing out good application. Application is the part of the talk that takes our core message and shows its significance in day-to-day living. It gives examples of what the teaching could look like in action, stirring people to consider what they might do differently as a result of what they have been hearing.

Pause:

Think back to the last talk you heard, or even gave. What was the application? Was it spelt out in the talk, or even hinted at through various illustrations? Can you see how the teaching was relevant to your everyday life? If not, how could that have been done differently?

As a speaker, it's not enough to just feel passionate about communicating a great biblical truth or theme – we should always be asking ourselves the question, 'Now what?' What would I love people to do as a result of hearing this talk? As we prepare our talks, we need to carefully consider what the practical implications to our message are. Why is it so important that our listeners get it? Why does this subject matter? How do we move from approving or agreeing with biblical truth to living out biblical truth? How could we as the Church develop in this area? What should our response be? What should we do?

As with other elements of a talk, the application should be tailored to the audience. Who are we addressing: Christians or non-Christians, old or young, married or single, family or no family, working or retired? The chances are there will be a combination of a number of these. Could the application look different depending on age and life-stage? We don't necessarily have to spell out an application for every people-group, but we should at least consider how it might vary from group to group. Another good question to ponder would be whether the talk calls for a corporate or individual response, or both.

And then having considered these questions we need to find ways to draw out the application and implications for our listeners. Here are some practical tips on how to do this in your talk:

- Give examples, ideas, illustrations, dreams or practical tips that show what it might look like to live in the light of your talk so that people have something to take away with them.
- You might choose to share how you and others have done the very thing you're talking about: what was easy, what wasn't; what worked and what didn't.
- Application should always include the everyday, and also the huge life-changing stuff. Don't be frightened of super-simple everyday examples − in fact these are often the best, giving people ideas that help them feel, 'I could do that.'
- The application doesn't need to be a set section − it can be littered throughout.
- Although there may be many different applications to your talk, as you prepare ask God to highlight the one thing he wants to emphasize; the one thing people can take away with them.

From time to time, there won't be a practical application for a talk. For example, Andy Croft did a series on Jesus in the Gospels. For one of these talks in particular, there was nothing practical to take away − the purpose of the talk was to bring us to a place of once again saying 'wow' at who Jesus is. So Andy was very upfront and said as much. He let us know there was no practical application − it was just about us gazing on Jesus and being in a place of wonder once again. When there is no practical application, let's not contrive something, let's just say so.

The Application in *O Come Let Us Adore Him*

The only application in this talk was: 'Let us adore him, let us worship him'.

We also need to remember that the Holy Spirit is the great applicator. He has a varied job description, which includes drawing us into all truth and changing us to be more like Jesus. So the good news is it's not all on our shoulders. Once we've done our job in preparing and delivering a talk, there's nothing better than leaving room for the Holy Spirit to do whatever he wants to do – including speaking to individuals about their personal response to what they've heard.

Pause:

Imagine you were preparing a talk on submission to God and to each other. Think about what submission might look like for your listeners (and yourself).

Interview

Right Reverend David and Mary Pytches

I love hearing both David and Mary teach. They are quite different in style, but they have an authority and wisdom which they've gained from a quite a few more years following Jesus and leading his people than many of us. I am so encouraged and challenged by their stories of how following Jesus works out in real life. They carry weight and depth as communicators, and bring God's Word to life with power, honesty, clarity, and a real sense of the Holy Spirit's life and breath.

Why do we preach? What do you understand the purpose of preaching to be?

David: Because we're told to preach the gospel. We want to tell people about Jesus who is the way to the Father. Our first objective is that people would come to Christ and be saved.

Mary: For me the purpose of preaching changes depending what's on my heart, what he has placed within me. He places different things in different people: for me personally, I especially want to see people grow and mature. I've read more about this subject than most others because it is something God has put on my heart.

Have you always wanted to speak? When did you know it was part of your calling?

David: It was more that I was called to leading a church, so I had to do it! And when I've got something to say, I'll say it.

Mary: I got a hint when I was converted and gave my testimony for the first time. An old lady came and told me that I was going to be a missionary. For many years that was buried in my psyche, as I had my family to look after. Then when I did begin speaking publicly, it was in Spanish! [David and Mary were missionaries in Chile.]

Can you remember the first talk you ever gave? If so, how did it go?

David: Yes, it was terrible. I really didn't know how to put a talk together, and didn't know how to say it. I'm a church-shaper rather than a preacher. I didn't have the right words and wasn't sure how to express myself. That comes with practice. I was comforted by Moses and Jeremiah in the Bible – they also felt very inadequate when God called them to speak.

Mary: Yes, I was at Bible college and I spoke on 'as having nothing and yet possessing all things' (2 Cor. 6:10, KJV). I didn't really know what I was talking about, but it seemed to go quite well. I was terribly nervous, but afterwards I thought, gosh, I really enjoyed that. Then I got married, babies followed and my desire to speak got buried. That was good, in a way, because when a seed is buried things happen. I had gained some experience of life, and had got to know myself better in the meantime.

Is there any part of talk preparation or delivery that you've particularly had to work on?

David: My weakness is that I tend to talk without organizing my material adequately. Mary sometimes asks me if I need to do more preparation for a talk, but I get to the stage where I don't dare look at it, because then I'll think of many more things to say. I keep praying about the talk and checking it over, but the more I do this, the more it grows and the more the stories come. So organization is something I've had to try to watch. But it is also important to be yourself. I know what I should do: I should tell the listeners what I'm going to say, say it, and then summarize what I've told them. I know I should do that, but I don't do it very well.

Mary: My problem is finding the right illustrations. I know I need them, but have always struggled to find them. Reading gives me most illustrations. Also, I don't want to give a condemning or negative talk. I want people to be encouraged, so sometimes I've had to alter my material to give the right emphasis. There needs to be a balance in that.

Who has inspired you as a speaker in the past, and who do you like to listen to now?

David: John Stott was my hero in my youth. Billy Graham, John Wimber, Eleanor Mumford (she delivers a talk beautifully) and Steve Nicholson.

Mary: Christine Perkin (I remember she did three extremely good studies on Gideon), Ele Mumford, and John Stott. John Wimber was also my hero. He was so real, brilliant at illustrating, very relaxed and a good Bible teacher. We should always be learning from others. If we speak regularly, we need to make sure we're also on the receiving end of talks.

How do you prepare your talks, and what is your starting point?

David: It often starts when praying and reading my Bible. I will underline something that strikes me and it grows from there. Also, hearing testimonies and reading Christian biographies fires me up. The problems people in the congregation have, or struggles in the wider Church, also trigger my train of thought.

Mary: I pray, 'Lord what is it you want me to tackle?' Usually it's something I've read that sparks something, or it's finding a passage that I love, something that has spoken to me. Sometimes it's a personal issue I've struggled with and I ask the Lord, 'How do I deal with this?' And in going through that process with God I then become an expert on it. I search for answers and can then pass on what I find. I also ask God for the 'now' book ('What should I be reading?') and that often sparks off the beginning of a talk idea.

What would you say is the most important element of a talk?

David: I think it's fire. You've got to feel the fire in your belly that you want people to catch. D.L. Moody had a church in Chicago in the nineteenth century. One night the church caught fire (even before the ashes had cooled he collected enough money for the repairs) and as the church burned he saw a friend in the crowd of onlookers who he'd been trying to get along to church for years. Moody asked why he had waited so long before coming to the church. The man's response was that he hadn't seen a church on fire before! It is the anointing of the Holy Spirit we desperately need so that we preach with fire and passion. And we need to keep asking God for this.

Mary: The doctrine or theological basis for what you're saying has to be right. Also illustrations – an illustration gives a model of how to do it – the 'how' is really important.

What would you say makes a good talk, good and a bad talk, bad?

David: A bad talk is when the speaker isn't saying anything; when it's boring waffle. If you don't strike oil in ten minutes, stop boring!

Mary: A bad talk has a lack of illustrations, and a lack of vulnerability in the speaker. Also, I can't bear it when a talk is read.

Can you think of any mistakes you've made, or problems you've had to overcome?

David: Yes! My struggle is timekeeping. And I have sometimes spoken on things too much beyond my own experience. I also had to learn not to condemn and speak to 'us' not 'you'.

Mary: Sometimes I think I've not prayed enough. We can always say that, but sometimes busyness means I haven't sought God enough. We have to seek God's anointing.

I've always tried to avoid leaving people thinking I was amazing. I want people to think Jesus is amazing, but sometimes the stories we tell in our preaching can give the impression that we've got it all together.

Is there a particular verse or subject you love to speak on again and again?

David: That God is always doing a new thing. God is living and always on the move, giving more life, grace and love – I like to speak on that. I also often return to the subject of not despising the day of small things.

Mary: Personal growth and wholeness. That's my passion.

Do you have any top tips for engaging an audience?

David: If you can see you're not connecting, ask the audience a question to help them engage with your material. That gets their attention. John Wimber used to say: 'I think it's time for a "ghost story"' (meaning the Holy Spirit).

Mary: Eyeball them! You have to have eye contact. Also, tell them a story, maybe something funny about a personal predicament.

David and Mary, together with their four daughters, spent seventeen years in South America as missionaries. When they returned to England they led the church of St Andrew's, Chorleywood and pioneered New Wine conferences (which later gave birth to Soul Survivor). Both David, a bishop, and Mary still minister around the world – David speaks and writes on renewal and leadership issues, while Mary is a popular speaker and author on issues of personal growth.

12.

Let Your Body Do the Talking – Body Language

Much of this book is intended to help us think about our words – ensuring we say what we actually mean to say. But a huge part of our communication isn't about the words we use, but our body language and our delivery:

* What we do with our bodies – posture, position, eye contact, gestures, movements and expressions.
* The way we speak – the quality of voice, accent, projection, emphasis, expression, pace, volume and pitch.

Our body language and delivery are a large proportion of our communication,[6] so we need to spend some time looking at these important elements. Though you won't use these skills until you actually come to deliver your talk, it's important you consider them, and if necessary practise them as part of your preparation.

Body Language

It's really easy to overlook the importance of what we do with our bodies when we speak. And yet when you think of speakers you find really engaging, the chances are they use their bodies well. Good body language makes for a much more engaging speaker, so let's take a look at three key areas to be especially aware of.

Stand

How we stand speaks volumes before you even begin. It lets the audience know whether we're comfortable and happy to be there, or nervous and lacking confidence. For example, leaning away from the audience says we don't really want to connect with them, whereas leaning slightly towards them says we want to engage with them and want to remove some of the distance between us and them. Audiences will always take on and receive these messages, though they do it without thinking, so we need to try to keep our bodies looking relaxed and informal, but engaging (a bit of a tall order):

- As you speak you can move around the stage, but remember to be still at times. Constant motion, such as swaying or pacing, is a distraction and can be annoying – beware of the caged-lion look.
- If you're moving around, it will usually be during a moment where you know your notes really well (often when telling a story). If this is the case, make sure you are back at your notes before coming to the end of the bit you know well, so you're not left with an awkward pause, while you desperately try to pick up your place in your notes.

- If you're using PowerPoint, try to ignore it. Trust it's there and keep looking at the audience – it's hard for them to engage with you if your back is turned to them.

A Note on What to Wear

As we prepare to speak, we need to pause and think about what to wear. Because no one appreciates a naked speaker. Actually there is probably a church out there somewhere called Church of the Nudey Dudies – if you're part of that movement please feel free to skip this section.

When we speak we don't want anything to detract from what we're communicating, and that includes what we wear, so it's good to think through a couple of basic questions:

- Who am I speaking to? Different churches and cultures have different approaches to dress. It would be hugely inappropriate to dress casually in some settings, and totally OK in others. Know your audience, and if in doubt, find out.
- Can I move freely in this outfit without fear of tripping up, and do I have my full range of movement (nothing too tight on the arms or legs)?
- If you're wearing jeans or trousers, is the zip secure? There's nothing worse than constantly worrying that you're flashing your undies. It's also distracting for your listeners if they're trying to meet your eye while their gaze drifts downwards.
- Do I feel comfortable in this? Trying a new look for the first time when speaking probably isn't the best idea – it could leave you feeling unnecessarily self-conscious.

- Is everything that should be covered, covered? And will it stay covered during the duration of my talk, including if I bend down to take a sip of water? A practical tip here: stand in front of a mirror. Check 1: Stretch right up high and check your midriff is still covered. Check 2: If you're a woman, bend down and check there's no cleavage on display. Check 3: Bend down again and check that anyone behind you (an unsuspecting band member, for example) doesn't get a flash of bum, or boxer shorts or knickers.

- Is this outfit easy on the eye or unnecessarily distracting? I'm not saying when speaking we should all be Plain Janes or Jims, but also we don't want people to be more fixated with our rainbow jodhpurs than with what we're bringing from the Word of God.

- Will I be too warm in this? Usually when we're speaking, the nerves (even low level), adrenaline and possible stage lighting will mean that our bodies are slightly hotter than usual, so don't wrap up too warmly.

Move

Most of us move our bodies (or parts of them – most commonly our hands) in normal everyday conversation – this should be the same when we speak:

- You *should* be using your hands – they shouldn't be in your pockets or behind your back.
- Don't use your hands to play with change, fiddle with your notes, or do anything else that might take the attention away from what you're saying.
- Instead your hands should be used as non-verbal punctuation, to help emphasize and express a point.

• When you're not gesturing, your hands should rest at your sides because this lets those listening know you're relaxed.

But it's not just our hands. Our gestures should be large enough to embrace the entire room full of people and appropriate to the size of the venue. This means that when speaking to a larger audience we might want to think about using more than just our hands. Big movements that come right from your shoulders shouldn't seem out of place on a big stage to a big crowd. Think about how to use your whole body to emphasize a point – hand gestures, wide expansive arms; crouching down low, reaching high.

You won't be at your most effective if you spend the entire talk hidden behind a lectern. Not only does this create a barrier between you and the audience, it will also hinder the amount you move. Try to have your notes slightly to one side, or make sure you come out from behind the lectern from time to time.

When it comes to using our bodies well, different things will work for different people, depending on our personality and how we communicate in everyday conversation. However, a word of caution: when this is overdone it will seem theatrical and could be uncomfortable for the audience. Be yourself, plus about 5 per cent. The way we use our bodies should be controlled and purposeful – erratic movements should be eliminated.

Pause:

Think about what sort of gestures you would naturally use when in conversation. Identify some and then try enlarging them. Give it a go in front of a mirror or a friend, and see what works for you.

Accessories and Minimizing Distraction

I love wearing chunky necklaces and have many in lots of different colours to go with any and every outfit. But I've learned the hard way that big necklaces and clip-on radio mics aren't best friends. There was an unfortunate bunch of people who had to sit through an entire talk nervously awaiting my next movement, and the ensuing amplified crash of wooden beads down the sound system. Lesson learned. If I'm speaking somewhere new and don't know what type of microphone I might end up with, then it's best to keep things simple with the accessories.

On another occasion I wore hot-pink wooden-bottomed shoes that looked cooler than they sound. They finished off my outfit nicely, but made a lot of noise on the wooden stage every time I moved. I now remember to think through footwear as well as the rest of my outfit.

So, male or female, take a moment to consider what you'll wear and you won't get caught out.

Express

Our facial expressions help communicate our feelings – anything from encouragement to concern. The most important element of facial expression is eye contact. This is so key because it gives our message credibility – showing we have integrity and honesty and that we are sincere in what we're saying. Again, we recognize this is true because if someone is chatting to us one-on-one we automatically feel suspicious or uncomfortable if they can't make eye contact with us. On the other hand we tend to find someone who can regularly meet our gaze engaging and interesting; we find ourselves wanting to hear more.

Pause:

To see the importance of eye contact for yourself, try a little experiment. Grab a friend and tell them a true story using no eye contact, then the same story with regular eye contact. Then get them to do the same to you. Note how you felt about both the story and the person communicating it.

Eye contact is one of the chief means we have of connecting with our audience, so we need to work on getting this right:

* Initially, if you are just too nervous you can fake it by looking above people's heads, but this isn't ideal.
* Give good eye contact with individuals, and ensure you are slow enough in your movements and your gaze to really engage one person at a time.
* If you do this you are much more likely to invite your listeners to look at you while you speak, which means you are more likely to hold their attention.
* It is quite common to give more eye contact to someone who is smiling at you, has an encouraging expression or whose opinion you particularly care about. Be aware of this and make sure you take in the whole of the audience, not just a few individuals.
* Give equal and regular attention to the left, the right and the centre of the room. In a traditional church building this is a lot easier than a more modern warehouse-style space, as the congregation are probably straight in front of you, rather than out to the sides. In either case, make sure you

avoid the 'Wimbledon look' – moving your eyes from extreme left, to extreme right, to extreme left, as though watching a game of tennis.

If you are nervous, you might find that your face freezes a little, so try to consciously relax – start by smiling, this will help you and your audience. Then try to remember to smile from time to time in your talk – again this will communicate that it's not all deep, heavy and serious, and will help people stay engaged.

We need to ensure our body language doesn't contradict what we are actually saying, e.g. don't shake your head when you're saying something positive, or fold your arms when talking about the welcoming love of God the Father. If we're telling people about good news then we should probably look reasonably happy, and if we're saying God's arms are open wide to us then perhaps our arms should also be open.

Do	**Don't**
Relax	Stand rigidly
Use your hands	Fiddle
Confirm what your're saying verbally	Contradict what you're saying verbally
Reach out to your audience in your gestures	Fold your arms
Move	Hide behind the lectern
Walk around in the stage	Pace
Have moments of stillness	Move constantly
Make eye contact	Avoid eye contact
Face the whole audience	Face one side or person
Slightly exaggerate movements	Overdo or ham-up movement
Smile	Look cross

The key to effective body language is to look natural even though it will probably require some work to use our bodies and our faces to connect with our listeners. We need to do all we can to keep them with us as we take them through the journey of our talk.

Pause:

Try preaching in front of a mirror, or even videoing yourself to see what you look like. What works and what needs improving? As in all things, don't try to tackle every weak area at once. Start by working on one or two elements and go from there.

13.

Bring It! – Delivery

The way we use our voice is hugely important in effectively communicating any message God has given us. We don't want to waste the great material that we have worked so hard on because of poor delivery. How we sound, whether we're too fast, too slow, too boring, if we mumble or shout, if we're monotone or breathy – all of this, and more, will impact our audience. It will affect their decision to stay tuned in to what we're saying, and their ability to receive the message.

Pause:

When it comes to being a more engaging speaker, it's great to listen to someone who really grabs you and ask yourself why – why does this work, what is so good, what do they do that holds my attention and that makes the time pass quickly? Is there anything you can take from their talk or style that you could adopt? Also, the next time you're bored or disengaged, ask yourself why, and work to eliminate those things in your own speaking.

One of the most important things we can do to help our listeners engage with our message is to sound interested and passionate. A monotone voice will cause people to tune out even if we're passing on the most amazing revelation ever from God's Word. The other elements covered in this book will not be effective unless we sound like we want to be there and are passionate about our topic. I remember when a friend of mine gave her first talk at church. She was speaking on her primary passion: worship. There are many things she could have done better. She didn't always know where she was in her notes, she didn't have the clearest structure to her talk and it was slightly too long. But she had everyone's attention throughout. Someone said to me afterwards that they actually found themselves leaning in, wanting to hear more. Why? Because she loves her subject. She loves worshipping God and wants everyone else to 'get it' too. Her passion was endearing, attractive and captivating. It wasn't a cross, angry passion. It was inviting. Her passion ensured her message came across. It was received, loud and clear. People will listen to passionate people.

Along the same lines, speaking faster communicates interest and passion. If we speak too slowly we could be perceived as dull and uninteresting, so if that is our tendency we need to speed up. People tend to think faster than we speak, so if we're not speedy our listeners will be one step ahead of us, having worked out where we're going. If this happens too consistently, they will struggle to stay engaged and could be driven mad by the delay in waiting for us to catch up with them. We need to find a pace that is quite . . . pacey. But, on the other hand, if we speak too fast people won't be able to understand what we're saying, and it will wear them out and frustrate them. It's not a great feeling to listen to a speaker when you feel like you're caught up in the eye of a storm.

Pause:

Listen back to the last talk you gave. If you find yourself wanting to press fast-forward then it's time to speed up. But if it's too speedy, work on slowing down next time. Ask someone else what they think as they'll probably be more objective than you. It's good for us to be aware of our speed.

It's not about finding one speed and switching on cruise control. Our speed, as well as our tone of voice and volume, should be varied during the course of our talk. A change of pace and pitch can be used to communicate excitement, seriousness or to emphasize a particularly critical point. A well-timed pause can draw people in, causing them to feel expectant of what's coming next. It also allows the listener time to process and take in the message and so keep up with you.

If these skills don't come naturally to you, then work to develop them. They are important. I've seen that women are often naturally better at this than the guys, if you will forgive the generalization. I think it's because of the way we communicate in our everyday lives and – watch out, here comes another generalization – we tend to be a bit more animated in this. Preaching is a type of performance. There must be energy, remembering that people will engage with us if we sound interested and interesting, if we sound like what we're saying is worth knowing, exciting and important. In 1675 the Archbishop of Canterbury asked an actor, Mr Butterton, about the ability actors had to affect an audience. 'Why, my Lord,' answered Butterton, 'the reason is very plain. We actors on the stage speak of things imaginary as if they were real and you in the pulpit speak of things real as if they were imaginary.' I think this is still a danger more than three hundred years on, so we must make sure we sound interested when speaking about the Bible and God's truth. We need to speak of things that are real, true and important with energy and life. (To be totally clear, authenticity matters, and when we speak it is so important that we are ourselves. I'm not in any way saying we should act a part or be someone we are not. Those listening to us will pick up quickly on a lack of authenticity, and it usually leads to cynicism or detachment.)

One thing I've noticed engaging speakers often have in common is a certain rhythm to their speaking at key moments, employing what are actually oratory techniques even though we don't necessarily notice them as such. One really effective technique is the power of threes. 'For yours is the kingdom, and the power and the glory, forever. Amen' is an example straight from the Lord's Prayer. Another example is, 'Jesus Christ is the same yesterday and today and forever' (Hebrews 13:8). This same pattern can be used to make a strong point: 'The cross speaks of his mercy, the cross speaks of his love, the cross speaks of his grace.' The power of threes is effective because it employs a rhythm that is pleasing to listen to and feels satisfyingly complete.

Don't Be Put Off

Don't be put off by sleepers or miserable-looking people – some people have bad listening faces. They're probably just concentrating – or at least tell yourself that to get you through to the end. I've had the best feedback from people who looked like they wanted to stone me – so decide in advance you're not going to let faces distract you.

Here are some ideas and examples to consider in your delivery:

- Try to avoid phrases such as 'this is so exciting, this is so important'. It is our job as communicators to show them why something is exciting or important, not simply to tell them it is. We need to put the truth in such a way that it will lead them to that conclusion themselves. Don't tell them what to think or feel. C.S. Lewis, theologian and author, once advised that, when writing, an author should avoid using adjectives which tell the reader how to feel about whatever is being described. Instead of saying something is 'terrible', it should be described so they will be terrified; don't say it was 'delightful', make them say 'delightful' when they've read the description. Lewis pointed out that adjectives of emotion are like asking someone else to do your job for you.[7] The same applies to teaching.
- Work to ensure your voice is loud and clear, and that your diction is good (no mumbling). A phrase I love, coined by Revd Dr Mike Lloyd, a theologian and communicator, is 'Go and get them with your voice', speaking of the need for us to draw people in with the way we use our voice, including being loud enough to engage and captivate attention.
- Try not to sound cross because this will place a barrier between you and your audience. We looked earlier at the importance of sounding passionate, but we need to remember that passion is not the same as anger or frustration. No one wants to be shouted at or bullied into believing something. Anger doesn't encourage people to listen, but instead can be quite offensive, making the listener feel uncomfortable and less likely to be open to the message. The exception to this is if you are cross about something on which they can agree with, for example, injustice. Passion that is hopeful and relational will draw people in; passion that is angry or frustrated repels.
- Watch the tone of your voice to ensure it is humble and inclusive. Try not to be arrogant or come across like a teacher speaking to pupils, but instead as one learner to

another. Nerves can do strange things, make people sound 'holier than thou', when that really isn't their heart. If that is your tendency, you will need to watch out, as it could put people off.

◆ Having said this, don't be afraid to speak with authority. Once you're properly prepared you should know, if nothing else, that your talk is biblical – it therefore carries authority, so you should communicate it accordingly.

◆ Speaking of nerves, they do all sorts of funny things to us and the chances are if they are noticeable in any way they will affect your delivery. Be aware of any nerve-induced weaknesses and try to eliminate or disguise them. You should speak with confidence, even if you feel anything but. It will help people relax and enjoy listening to you. Watch for anything that might distract your listeners – dry mouth or breathiness are two classics, and both are usually down to nerves. If you get a dry mouth, make sure you have water with you (but don't sip it every two minutes, as that can be just as distracting). If, like me, you tend to get breathy when nervous, then use the few moments before you speak to take some really good deep breaths, remembering to both exhale as well as inhale. (Failure to do both elements of the whole breathing malarkey could mean you hyperventilate or pass out, neither of which will help you.) Also if you find you develop a nervous cough when speaking, remember not to do it into the microphone.

◆ If your voice is too harsh, soft or breathy, and you can't seem to correct it on your own, consider having one or two sessions with a vocal coach.

◆ Work at sounding natural, avoiding using a fake 'speaker's voice' as much as possible. The more a talk has become part of you (not a script learned, but a subject mulled over and connected with) the easier this will be.

◆ Be careful of using formal or written language such as 'furthermore' or 'and so to conclude this talk'. This is a particular danger if you write your talks out in full (which in general is a great idea).

* Always practise your talk out loud. This will enable you to spot unnatural-sounding sentences and become very familiar with your content. If you are too dependent on your notes, you will read from them, which is not very captivating. Also you won't be able to make eye contact, which means the level of engagement will be even worse. I was listening to a talk some while ago where the speaker read entirely from their notes, barely glancing up between sentences. It was such a shame. His material was good, but people weren't giving him their attention, as he didn't sound (or look) interesting or engaging.

* Pauses can be powerful, so make sure you use them from time to time. They help to draw your listeners in, enable them to capture and digest what they've just heard, or catch up if their mind has wandered. Don't use them too much as the talk will become laboured, but use them after making a key point, reading from the Bible or reading a quote.

* You also need to make sure you know how to handle a microphone. If you're speaking somewhere for the first time, then check with the sound engineer how to hold the microphone as they vary and might require a different technique to what you're used to.

* Look out for, and eliminate, bad habits such as 'you know', 'sort of', 'kind of thing', 'umm', 'like', etc. If you're not sure whether you're a culprit, listen to a recording of you speaking, or ask someone to count how many times you use these non-phrases in a talk.

* Finish your sentences, and don't overly repeat or labour a point – do it well then move on.

As speakers we need to decide to be ourselves and not an imitation of another speaker. However, it's important that we polish and grow our gift so that we become the best communicator we possibly can be. This process won't always be easy or comfortable, but it will pay off, helping us to effectively communicate whatever God has led us to say.

Rhetorical Questions

If you are going to ask a rhetorical question in your talk, make it clear that you're not expecting an answer from your audience. If you are asking a genuine question, and are expecting audience participation, make that clear too. It is important that people feel safe as they are listening to you and that people don't do the wrong thing and feel embarrassed, so either way let them know.

Pause:

If you can, find someone to pair up with for this pause. Person number one look up Matthew 13:1–9, the Parable of the Sower. Person number two should find Luke 15:11–20, the story of the Lost Son. Alternatively, you can each choose your favourite Bible story. Both people should take a few minutes to read the story through a couple of times. Then take it in turns to tell that story to your partner, in no more than five minutes. This is not necessarily about learning the passage by heart – you can keep the Bible open for help, but tell it in your own words. Don't preach on the passage, just tell it in the most engaging way you can. As you listen to your partner, keep an ear out for what helps you engage and keeps you interested in the story. Then give feedback and swap over.

Interview

Mike Pilavachi

I have had the privilege and enjoyment of working with Mike for many, many years and have learned so much from him. As I've watched him in action, on stage and off, I've learned the importance of great illustrations and genuine humility, and that good talks always start with a passion for God and his people. Mike is not only a world-class communicator, but a faithful and encouraging friend.

Why do we preach? What do you understand the purpose of preaching to be?

The purpose is to communicate two things that seem different, but are actually very similar: God's truth (his mind) and God's love (his heart). Preaching should reveal both. At its best, preaching should inform the mind and warm the heart. What we, as communicators, have to do is to be faithful to God's Word, not preaching our opinions or good ideas, but teaching his truth. The prerequisite is we have to be in his Word. This doesn't mean that we should be quoting vast chunks of Scripture, but we do have to show where we have drawn our teaching from. The best preaching is revelatory – it opens people's eyes. Too often people preach what is already known, but preaching is at its best when it is prophetic – where it leaves people with a sense of 'eureka!' and something happens as a result of that revelation. When we hear and receive revelation we love God more, and when we love God more, our life changes – the purpose of preaching is, more than anything, to do that.

Have you always wanted to speak? When did you know it was part of your calling?

Fairly soon after becoming a Christian, I longed to preach, though I never thought I would or could. When I was 16, whenever I came across a truth in God's Word, I would imagine teaching that discovery to others. And I wouldn't just imagine it – I would preach it to my friends. I distinctly remember being on the London Underground with a friend of mine. We discussed passionately what the letter to the Romans meant, what it meant to be dead to sin. I loved it! And so for me, it was not about standing in front of lots of people and preaching, it's more that I've never been able to keep myself from telling others. If I discover a good TV series I want to share it. If I discover a good meal I want to share it. And even more, if I discover a wonderful truth about Jesus, I want to share it, I want to tell someone.

Can you remember the first talk you ever gave? If so, how did it go?

Yes. My lip quivered and my knees shook all the way through it. It was on what it means to love each other, the new commandment. And to my mind it was an astounding success, simply because I got to the end, but I have no idea what anyone else thought of it.

Is there any part of talk preparation or delivery that you've particularly had to work on?

In terms of preparation, I constantly have to work on preparing properly. Life is very busy and so there is sometimes the temptation to work on my talk even as I'm giving it. This is not recommended! God is very gracious, and sometimes a point or illustration comes into my head as I'm giving the talk, but again this is not how it should be. I need to make more time for the part of the preparation where I feel I've got nothing! That's the process of waiting on God.

For two to three years, I did a show on Premier Radio. After a few shows, one of the senior producers took me aside and said she needed to train me on how to speak. She took a recording of one of my shows and played it to me twice. The first time was a straight recording with no adjustments. The second recording was a cleaned up version: all of the 'ums', 'errs', 'likes', and 'you knows' removed. When I heard the recordings back-to-back it was a revelation, it was life-changing. In the first unadjusted version, I had to concentrate to hear the message, in the second I actually sounded quite eloquent.

Who has inspired you as a speaker in the past, and who do you like to listen to now?

Basil Fawlty, Eric Morecambe, John Wimber, Tony Campolo, J.John and President Bartlett (a fictional character in The

West Wing) have all been an inspiration to me for a whole variety of reasons.

Currently, I love listening to people like Timothy Keller because he communicates deep truths, using great illustrations without excess waffle, and I don't feel as though I'm wasting any of my time – every word counts. There are one or two speakers out there who speak for an hour and at the end of their talk, I realize they could have said the same message in twenty minutes. I find myself wanting the other forty minutes back.

How do you prepare your talks, and what is your starting point?

I have to allow time for talks to gestate. Over the past six months or so, I've been on a wonderful journey looking at the subject of the Trinity, at how God is relational, and reflecting on the curse of individualism in the light of that. Every few days, I come across something in the Bible, or someone says something, or a thought comes to me, and I think, 'Oh my goodness! Yes, that's it!' And I feel like I'm seeing something in a completely different way.

Preparing a talk is a bit like preparing to give birth. Where I go wrong is I often induce labour and give birth to a talk before it has gone full-term. When a talk is very premature it comes out weak, sickly and insipid, and everyone wonders if it's going to survive. Sometimes I need to have the discipline to wait until a talk is ready; at that point there is what some people would call an anointing on that talk. I need the discipline to allow a talk to gestate.

I often have three, four or five different things going on in my life, in my head, and in my heart. I don't sit down in a study and write, but I'm constantly thinking, using every spare moment in a plane, car, in bed, or in conversation. I'm not recommending this as a right approach. I wish I had the discipline, and the time, to go through the agony of barrenness that leads to the longing to give birth, and the joy of when it arrives.

So talk preparation is a bit like giving birth (not that I know a lot about that!).

What would you say is the most important element of a talk?

I often try to think to myself before I give a talk: what is the main thing I want to leave people with? What is the practical thing that can change in their lives when they put it into practice? Or, what is the one truth they can respond to in worship, and as a result love Jesus more?

What would you say makes a good talk, good and a bad talk, bad?

The sign of a good talk is, after it's over, can I remember it? My friend, worship leader and songwriter Matt Redman used to say that the genius of songwriting is to write about universal truths in a unique way. And I think that's not a bad motto for preachers too. We should seek to put universal truths in a unique way, so that people receive revelation that they can remember and take into their week. And that happens if as speakers we're disciplined to hone our message – that we identify the thing we want to drive home.

A bad talk is where there is no revelation, or where the speaker says all the right things, but says them in such a way no one can remember them.

Can you think of any mistakes you've made, or problems you've had to overcome?

My good friends have told me that I'm at my worst when I try to say too much. I try to fit too much in and then people end up with nothing. Too often I've gone ten minutes over time because I didn't have the discipline to hold back. I've seen people's eyes glaze over and I've realized I've lost them – they can't take any more. When I do this it dilutes the whole message. If I'd stopped ten minutes earlier, they would have heard more. Less is more, sometimes, and I'm trying to learn that.

Is there a particular verse or subject you love to speak on again and again?

Yes. I love to speak about God's sovereignty in our desert times. How he takes our weaknesses, our failures, our struggles, our dark nights of the soul, and out of them brings grace, strength and victory, with compassion, tenderness and care. Finding God in the desert places is a lifetime message for me.

Do you have any top tips for engaging an audience?

The way we communicate in most church settings – where someone gets up and speaks at other people for a certain amount of time – is only done in three other settings as far as I know. The first is the university lecture, the second is the political speech, and the third is the stand-up comedy routine. Most preaching and teaching is based on the university lecture: large on facts and original Greek. Some preachers go for great oration, like a political speech, that rouses people. But of the three, the person who influences society the most is, for me, the stand-up comedian. While they get you to laugh, they are giving you their perspective on life. They remind you of what you already know, that's why you resonate and identify with them. Some comedians have strong agendas and drive them home even as they're making us laugh. I've tried to base how I speak more on John Cleese than Tony Blair or David Cameron. I know not everyone wants to tell lots of jokes, and a talk doesn't have to be laugh-out-loud funny, but it does need to be human. Sometimes the university lecture is about getting across facts, regardless of whether people are really listening. A talk needs to be more than that. It needs to be authentic and human, even more than it needs to be funny.

Mike is the founder and director of Soul Survivor, a charity based in Watford that seeks to reach, encourage and equip young people to live their whole lives for Jesus. Soul Survivor runs events each summer which attract around thirty-thousand young people. Mike spends much of his time travelling and speaking at events all over the world. He is also the Senior Pastor of Soul Survivor Watford church. Mike has written a number of books, cooks the most extravagant barbecues, and is a little bit passionate about the vines he nurtures in his garden.

14.

Every Second Counts – Timing

A few years ago, one of the topics I spoke on regularly was depression. Having suffered with the illness myself for a while, I had a passion to encourage others who were going through something similar. A friend asked me to come and speak to their church on this topic, so I took with me my standard hour-long seminar. About forty minutes in, I started to wonder why people were fidgeting in their seats and no longer making eye contact, staring mindlessly – perhaps, desperately – at the floor. Ignoring the not-too-subtle warning signs, I kept ploughing through my prepared notes until the full hour of teaching was up. It wasn't until many months after that it finally occurred to me that firstly, I hadn't asked how long I should teach for; secondly, a whole hour of teaching might be more than was required in a church service; and thirdly, perhaps I wasn't interesting enough – nor the topic applicable enough – to take up a full sixty minutes of everyone's time. So this begs the question: when we preach, how long should it take?

This will largely depend on where we're speaking and what is asked of us. Don't leave it to your own ill-fated guesswork like I did. Find out in advance how long you should be, and stick to it. Timing is not necessarily just about people's attention span.

If we speak really well we might be able to engage an audience for an hour or more, but it's about doing what has been asked of us, coming under the authority of whoever has invited us to speak, and serving the rest of the service. For example, in the morning service of the church I attend, if a speaker takes too long then we've seen that parents grow tense about being late to collect kids, and they also miss out on an opportunity to respond in prayer or worship after the talk. We have also found that when a talk runs too long, then times of prayer ministry and waiting on God suffer (which for us at Soul Survivor is one of our highest priorities). Also the congregation have already given their attention for long enough and now want to do something else.

Here are some more top tips on timing:

- Rehearse your talk at least once before you give it, as this will help ensure you really do stick to time. Bear in mind that most people speed up when nervous.
- Try to make sure you give the right amount of time to the right section of your talk, not rushing one part or spending too long on a less important section. There is nothing worse than the first two points being really detailed, then having to skim through the last two sections, with little or no application to any of it because time ran away with you.
- On a very practical note, make sure you can see a clock. Not realizing you've gone over time should never be an excuse. I know of a few churches that have a big digital clock on the back wall of the church, counting down until the allocated time runs out – it's not a bad idea, and I reckon they would have hugely appreciated such a device halfway in to my depressing depression monologue.
- If you're giving a long talk, where it can be harder to keep track of time, think about giving yourself a rough guide at the bottom of each page, showing what the time should be for each section so that you continually know whether or

not you're on target, e.g. page 1 – 11.35 a.m., page 2 – 11.40 a.m., etc.

A final word on timing comes from an unknown contributor: 'The mind can only handle what the butt can endure.' Nicely put.

Pause:

Do you know how many words, or pages of notes, equals a twenty-five-minute talk for you? If not, get hold of any previous talks you've given and look at how long you spoke for. Compare that time to your notes and try to get a good idea of what your words equal in minutes. Use this as a rough guide for future preparation.

15.

Coming into Land: Ending Your Talk

My boss, Mike, is well known for a certain phrase: 'I'm just coming into land', meaning he is nearing the end of his talk. Usually (and I say this with huge amounts of respect) this sentence cannot be trusted. When he uses it, what he probably means is: 'I've just noticed the time and I really ought to be finishing up, but I've got a few more things to say. Just so you don't think I'm unaware of the time, I'll tell you that I'm coming into land, but in actual fact we'll be here a while longer.' What Mike fails to realize is that none of us were bothered by him coming to a close anyway – most people can listen to Mike talk for hours.

But the 'coming into land' phrase is actually a good one to consider when thinking about ending a talk. Think about the terminology. When a plane comes into land it does so slowly and gradually, rather than just dropping out of the sky. The passengers on board are given warning of the plane's descent, and have a chance to prepare themselves for their arrival.

In the same way we need to give careful thought as to how we bring our talk to a conclusion – slowly and gradually, rather than ending abruptly; giving our listeners warning of what is about to happen rather than leaving them feeling blindsided, or as though they've just crashed into the tarmac.

In my experience, the ending tends to be the least thought through part of many talks, but we need to make sure we work on it as much as we would our introduction or any other part. All too often a speaker comes to the end of his or her material, realizes they haven't thought through how to end and either simply stop, or fail to stop – circling the runway for many more frustrating and wasted minutes.

Instead of falling into either of those traps, we want to find a way to bring the talk to a close in a clear and memorable way, letting people know that the end is nigh (don't say 'finally' unless you mean it). Here are some tips on how to prepare your audience for landing:

- Slow down.
- You might want to summarize your content, reminding your listeners of what they've heard without introducing any new material.
- You could go back to your opening thought, question or statement.
- If you started with a strong illustration, you might want to return to it now you're at the end.
- Don't keep repeating what you've already said. Say what you want to say, then stop.
- Think through in advance how you will lead into the next part of the service: will there be an opportunity to respond in prayer or worship or by receiving ministry? If so, who is going to lead that and if it's not you, how will you hand over to the person who will be leading the response?

I've heard it said that when it comes to singing in a choir, the most important thing is that the singers start together and end together. Of course, if the middle bit is a complete mess there isn't much that can redeem the experience for the listener, but otherwise a strong beginning and a strong end go a long way. So give some careful thought, next time you speak, as to how you might 'come into land'.

Coming into Land in *O Come Let Us Adore Him*

I ended *O Come Let Us Adore Him* by simply recapping my main point – whether we are more like the shepherds or the Magi, let us worship him.

Pause:

If you have spoken previously, review the endings of those talks to see how you came into land. Is it something you have given enough thought to? The next time you hear a talk, listen to how the speaker comes to a conclusion and reflect on whether or not it was effective.

Interview

Ness Wilson

Ness was the first person I heard speak on how to improve our communication, and so she is indirectly responsible for this book. She sparked in me a way of thinking about, and developing in, my own communication that I then wanted to share with others. One thing I appreciate about Ness's speaking style is how clear she is in communicating the truth of God's Word worked out in real life, and I love the way she always has a fresh take on things.

Why do we preach? What do you understand the purpose of preaching to be?

We preach to connect and apply God's timeless Word to our particular community. I also believe we should always preach for change, in some way, however small. Our listeners should never go away unchanged.

Have you always wanted to speak? When did you know it was part of your calling?

I always loved being asked to do the reading in church as a child and a teenager and, when asked, I would practise reading the passage out loud, over and over again, until it was almost memorized, and then read the passage with great emphasis. It is only looking back I realize that was an indication of a desire to speak publicly. At the time I didn't recognize it as that. I began to consider it could be part of my future as a student, when I started to do very informal equipping sessions for other Christian students and really enjoyed speaking. On my degree course, I would also happily volunteer to be the group presenter of our projects, and would often set myself the challenge of keeping everyone's attention when presenting pretty tedious facts and figures.

Can you remember the first talk you ever gave? If so, how did it go?

The first talk I really remember giving in church was on prayer, to about seven people, and I remember really enjoying the preparation and delivery. I think my friends were surprised how good it was.

Is there any part of talk preparation or delivery that you've particularly had to work on?

I used to only feel I could give a certain talk to believers and a different one to seekers. I now feel strongly that every talk can both build believers and connect with seekers, but the confidence and skills to do that have only come to me in recent years. I have also had to be very intentional with finding, filing and using good stories, quotes and illustrations to add to the content of my talks, and I think my talks today are much richer for that than they were historically.

Who has inspired you as a speaker in the past, and who do you like to listen to now?

Elaine Storkey inspired me as she was one of the few really good female speakers I knew. In terms of gifted communicators I intentionally observed and learned from, I would say Jeff Lucas, Pete Gilbert, and in recent years, Bill Hybels.

How do you prepare your talks, and what is your starting point?

I get a blank sheet of paper, write the title at the top, and then dream or imagine what I want to see happen, or feel God wants to do as a result of my talk. I will then write down two or three statements of my 'end result'.

This then gives me a rise of faith about the impact of my talk, and this infuses the next stage of deciding on content and flow.

What would you say is the most important element of a talk?

Probably the first two minutes, as you either connect people to you and your message, or you lose them. I live with the line: 'You only get one chance to make a first impression.'

What would you say makes a good talk, good and a bad talk, bad?

A good talk is good when people go away being inspired, equipped or encouraged in their relationship with God. A bad talk can be bad for many reasons – too long, boring, irrelevant.

Can you think of any mistakes you've made, or problems you've had to overcome?

I used to speak too fast and literally get out of breath, which didn't help in clear communication. I've learned to slow down, vary my pace, and breathe.

Is there a particular verse or subject you love to speak on again and again?

The father heart of God and our identity in Christ – it seems to end up in many of my talks, regardless of the title.

Do you have any top tips for engaging an audience?

Smile lots, use eye contact well and self-disclose – people really like it when speakers are real, authentic and we 'tell on ourselves'. People often have to 'buy into you' before they will buy into your message, so anything that connects them to your humanity will help engage an audience.

Ness lives in a community house with her husband Rich, her two daughters, and two friends. She and a few friends started Open Heaven Church in Loughborough eighteen years ago when they graduated from the university there. She is team leader of the leadership team and also speaks at various events and conferences around the UK. Her passion is to see local churches flourish, moves of God among students, and women realizing how courageous they really are.

16.

Get Ready, Get Set –
Before You Give Your Talk

After lots of prayer, study, hard work, serious concentration and probably moments of utter frustration, you've done it. Your talk is complete. Well done! But before you actually deliver the talk, here are a few key things that are worth checking through:

Speak the Talk Out Loud

Do this at least once (preferably more). I often find that doing so gives me a new expectancy of what God wants to do through the talk, which then stops me from feeling daunted and instead begins to excite me. Speaking your talk out loud also enables you do several other things:

* Check it doesn't run over time.
* Spot any weak areas, lifeless sections, sentences that don't make sense, words or phrasing that sound too 'written' (e.g. 'and so, in conclusion, I would like to say. . .') and need a more relaxed, conversational approach instead, and sections that are too long or laboured.

- Note down anywhere you need to pause to enable people to take a point in, the points you particularly want to emphasize, and places where you might need to slow down.
- Get the talk 'in' you so that you're not too notes-dependent.

When we can speak a message from our heart, rather than our notes, it shows our listeners that it's important and that it's worth listening to. So even if we need notes, which many of us do (I am convinced this will probably always be the case for me, and am slightly envious of people who can do a talk note-free), we must never read from them. Referring to our notes from time to time, rather than reading from them, will also make for a more engaging talk.

Preparing Your Notes

- Prepare good notes. When you're learning, I recommend writing out talks in full. This stops you from going down a route you don't want to go, or confusing yourself mid-talk.
- Make sure your notes are clear and easy to read.
- Number the pages of your notes, so even if you drop them at the last minute there is no need to panic about the order.
- Print in a typeface big enough to see from a distance, with good line breaks so that words stand out from the page, and with page breaks in the right place (i.e. not mid-sentence, story or illustration).
- Highlight your talk using different colours (or use different fonts) so that key points, phrases, quotes and stories jump off the page, helping you to be less

notes-dependent. I always write my stories in green –
that way when I glance down and see the green, I
know I can leave my notes and enjoy the story. I write
the Bible in red, and quotes in blue.
* Write helpful pointers in the margin: e.g. slow down,
breathe, pause, look left/right.

Go Through Your Talk with Someone Else

Having done your talk out loud to yourself and made any
changes, it's then a really good idea to go over it with another
person. This will not only help you see if the talk has become
part of you, but also they will probably be able to spot what
you have missed (lack of clarity, lack of illustration, too much
jargon, skewed theology, etc.). Obviously, I hope that reading
and studying this book will do most of the work for you, but we
all have our blind spots. Going through your talk with someone
else is the communicator's equivalent of 'Does my bum look
big in this?' and you should do this when you've pretty much
finished your preparation, otherwise there is less to critique
and the exercise won't be as effective. Having said this, do
remember that it can be really helpful to chat your talk through
with others at earlier stages, especially if – like me – you do
your best thinking out loud.

Let There Be Lightness

A while ago, I went to a women's conference where
Mary Pytches was speaking in the two main sessions. In
the session directly after lunch my friend and mentor,
Prue Bedwell, was giving a seminar and it was hilarious:

a talk on friendship, littered with amusing anecdotes and laugh-out-loud stories. It was a really fun talk – not heavy in the slightest and it contained minimal 'teaching'. It was light – great for the 'siesta slot', and worked perfectly alongside the other main sessions, which were by nature a bit meatier and heavier. I spoke to Prue about this and she told me this was the plan. When Mary had asked Prue to speak, she specifically told her to have lots of fun to provide balance to the day.

This shows on a macro scale (a day conference) what is actually very important for the micro (an individual talk): meatier material is more palatable if there are lighter things to nibble on too. There needs to be balance. If a talk is too dry and serious, and full of information and exposition, then the listeners may tune out or fall asleep. Lighter moments created by illustrations and humour are essential in keeping your audience with you, and ensuring the talk is palatable. J.John uses the analogy of the sugar coating on a tablet that ensures we don't spit out the bitter pill. Humour and light moments in our talk will ensure people can swallow and digest the good, life-bringing truths we are bringing to them.

Pause and Consider

At this stage it isn't too late to pause and consider a few final things:

- If you haven't already done so, stop and think about any non-Christians who may be there when you give your talk, which will hopefully be the case. Will your talk leave them with questions that may need answering (even if briefly) within your talk? Is there a way to include the gospel message?

- Do one final check for any material that doesn't serve your 'one thing'. If there is, it's not too late to get rid of it.
- Be aware of anything you might be sharing that could cause a strong reaction in people or could leave you feeling vulnerable afterwards, or could mean that people want to share their stories with you. When I used to speak quite a bit on two subjects – singleness and depression – both were approached from a fairly personal angle. The first time I spoke on depression and shared my story, I felt very exposed afterwards and it stirred up a lot of bad memories for me. I needed someone to pray for me, followed by a good nap. One of the first times I spoke on singleness, I realized that in a room of about a thousand people, I didn't know anybody. Not only was I single, but in that moment I was also friendless. It was not a good realization, and definitely a lesson learned: don't do this alone. It's worth thinking through in advance how you might handle comments people make, questions they might have, and the way that sharing something personal might make you feel. And remember – once you've shared something publicly you can't take it back.
- Check that you can sum up your talk in one sentence. If you still can't do this, then the chances are you haven't yet fully got to grips with what you want to say. In which case, more work is needed.
- Think about what you would like the outcome of the talk to be. Envision it and pray into it.
- As you prepare to give a talk, do be aware of spiritual attack. Be alert, as 1 Peter 5:8 says. Know what your weak spots are and guard against them. I found that very commonly before giving a talk I would feel insecure about my friendships, bizarrely convinced that all my friends were talking about me behind my back. After this happened a few times, I finally cottoned on to the fact that the devil was trying to undermine me. I rebuked the devil and he fled (Jas 4:7). The enemy seems to rely on us being ignorant

or oblivious to his schemes, so we need to be aware that we do actually have an enemy and then cover our vulnerable bits. This also applies after we've given a talk.

When You're About to Speak

♦ Check you have what you need in advance: water, a stand for your notes, a clock/watch, and minimize distractions (e.g. close a window if there is a lot of noise outside).
♦ Make sure you've eaten something (unless you're too nervous) so you don't get light-headed.
♦ Check your stand is the right height before you start.
♦ Take a deep breath and go for it.

Finally, ask someone who is going to be there when you give your talk to be listening with a view to giving you feedback. Do this in advance so they are prepared. This person doesn't need to be a speaker, just someone who will be kindly honest – you could give them the checklist at the end of this chapter to show them what to look out for.

Pause:

When you come to the end of all your preparation, have a look at the final checklist and ensure you've considered each of the major things we've covered in this book. It may be that having checked over some of these pointers there is a little bit more work to be done. This can be frustrating when you thought you'd finished, but honestly, it is much better to put in the extra time now rather than kick yourself afterwards.

Final Checklist

Pray	– before, during and after.
Bible	– come from the Bible with what to say, and use it well.
Focus	– what is your main thing, what do you want God to say and do?
Introduction	– this is your key opportunity to connect.
Structure	– find a way to lead people through your material.
Illustrations	– bringing your talk to life in real and memorable ways.
Quotes	– short, relevant and on the screen.
Jargon	– make sure the language is inclusive.
Application	– what do they do with what they've heard?
Coming in to land	– don't give your audience whiplash.
Body Language	– communicate with your body as well as with words and eliminate anything weird or annoying.
Delivery	– keep your audience engaged.
Multimedia	– use it well.
Timing	– time yourself and stick to it.
Feedback	– ask someone in advance.

Interview

Tim Hughes

Tim is a hugely gifted worship leader and songwriter. Part of the territory that has come with Tim's calling is to teach about worship and to train other worship leaders. Tim has taken this very seriously, and over the years has become a great speaker. I know there will be some reading this book who feel that their primary calling lies elsewhere but, as with Tim, speaking is part of the territory. Even if speaking isn't your main focus, it is possible to excel with hard work, and I hope you'll find what Tim has to say really helpful.

Why do we preach? What do you understand the purpose of preaching to be?

I believe we preach because it is important to proclaim truth. The Bible says we shall know the truth and the truth shall set us free [see John 8:32]. God has gifted men and women to study and understand the Word, to bring it to life for everyday people, in a way that inspires them in their everyday walk. The main way we understand and learn about the character of God and the person of Jesus Christ is through the Bible. To have this explained on a weekly basis, in a practical, relevant and informative way, breathes life into people. For me, personally, my faith has grown hugely through the input and teaching of others. This shouldn't be at the expense of our own personal study, but obviously some people have a particular gift to really understand what God is saying through a particular passage, to capture the culture and the times, and to challenge God's people to make a stand. Preaching the truth has such power to heal, to stir, to envision and to transform.

Have you always wanted to speak? When did you know it was part of your calling?

I have actually shied away from the speaking. It is not something that has felt like a natural gift. I've always felt much safer hiding behind a guitar, but I think there comes a point when God has taught you stuff, and you have a passion and a vision that you want to share and communicate with others. I guess I've realized there are different styles of preaching, and not everyone has to be the dynamic, charismatic, funny communicator. Some of us can perhaps proclaim truth in a simple, matter-of-fact way, and there is still great power in that.

Can you remember the first talk you ever gave? If so, how did it go?

The first talk I ever gave was at a church in South Africa. I remember being absolutely terrified and spending hours practising in front of a mirror. In the end it went

OK. I'm sure it was actually pretty awful, but the people were very encouraging and kind.

Is there any part of talk preparation or delivery that you've particularly had to work on?

For me, the area of talk preparation that I have to work on is the theological study – to understand and unpack what I am trying to say. I think it is important to learn and digest what you want to say. It sounds obvious, but sometimes we can have a half-formed idea that we fail to fully research before we start communicating it. The danger is that we end up getting confused and convoluted. The time studying, and trying to grapple and understand the subject, both intellectually and spiritually, is very important and something I definitely still need to work on.

On a practical level, other things I have had to develop, in terms of my preparation, are the pace of delivery, finding lots of stories and anecdotes, and carefully planning and developing moments of humour that keep people engaged. These are important hooks that when used effectively, first and foremost bring understanding and insight into a particular theme, but also very much help to keep people attentive and interested. For me, I definitely have to work hard at keeping people interested in what I'm communicating.

Who has inspired you as a speaker in the past, and who do you like to listen to now?

Lots of people have inspired me as a speaker. Mike Pilavachi, Louie Giglio, Francis Chan, Tim Keller – these guys have an unbelievable way of communicating. You are absolutely gripped by their every word. However, someone who is perhaps one of the best teachers I have ever sat under is Nicky Gumbel. His research is so thorough and his delivery so clear and concise that you come away feeling like you have learned so much. He has definitely been a real role-model on how to prepare and deliver a talk.

How do you prepare your talks, and what is your starting point?

When preparing a talk I spend lots of time reading, thinking and talking to people. My starting point is usually the one key thing that I want to communicate, and then it is about backtracking into finding stories and illustrations, fleshing out the point, and shaping the journey to get people to that final moment where they realize what you are trying to say.

What would you say is the most important element of a talk?

For me, every great talk should have an action point or something we can do in response, whether it is a time of ministry or something that people can think about throughout their week, so they can start to put into practice some of the truths we have been proclaiming.

What would you say makes a good talk, good and a bad talk, bad?

I think a good talk is where a very simple message is being proclaimed in a very effective way. Perhaps the point is being hammered home from different angles, different illustrations and biblical truths.

A bad talk is when you end up going on a long, meandering journey – a lot of waffle and no clear structure. You get to the end and think, 'What on earth was that about?' Also, the truth is, in today's culture, you might have some great things to say, but if they're not delivered in an interesting and engaging way, then people just switch off. Delivery is extremely important.

Can you think of any mistakes you've made, or problems you've had to overcome?

The problem that I have had to overcome is a lack of confidence. I have found it has helped me hugely to speak the talk out three or four times before I deliver it. I'm not one of these people who can speak articulately off the cuff, so to spend time thinking through sentence structure, flow, delivery, pace of delivery, is really important. Maybe speaking it through to a friend helps. Also, listening back after a talk, it is fascinating to hear what you actually sound like. I have been helped hugely by having a few people who take extensive notes on my delivery to feed it back – things such as throwaway words or nervous habits that can distract.

Is there a particular verse or subject you love to speak on again and again?

The subject I love to speak on again and again is worship: releasing people to worship God, understanding what worship is and the importance of it in transforming the Church. I will never get tired of speaking on that.

Do you have any top tips for engaging an audience?

Start with a very strong story. Make sure you know exactly what your first sentence will be. If you start poorly, it can be hard to regain people's attention. Also, I think it is extremely important to end well. Again, perhaps with a powerful story that moves people and unpacks everything you are trying to explain. Whenever I look through my teaching, for every key message and point I am trying to communicate, I always want to have one story or something funny that keeps people listening – people switch off so easily. Also, it's much better to speak brilliantly for fifteen minutes than to do an average talk for thirty minutes. When it comes to communicating, I personally believe in quality above quantity every time.

Tim started leading worship as a teenager at the Soul Survivor festivals. He eventually became director of worship at Soul Survivor Watford before moving to London in 2005 to take on the responsibility of overseeing worship at Holy Trinity Brompton, one of the largest churches in the UK. Tim also co-leads Worship Central, a school of worship designed to encounter God, equip the worshipper and empower the local church. Tim has written many well-known worship songs such as Here I am to Worship *and* Beautiful One. *He is married to Rachel, and they have three children, Phoebe, Simeon and Lois.*

17.

Pray Continually –
Seeking God Throughout

Early on we looked at how prayer should be our starting point in preparing a talk. But we really need to be calling out to God throughout the process. We need the leading of the Spirit in our preparation and speaking as we look to bring a message from God that ignites passion, perseverance, growth, change and dependence on him. We are going to need his help in doing this.

Ask God:

- What to speak on (or how to speak into a specific subject).
- What he wants to do through your talk.
- For insight into his Word, asking him how to bring his truth to life.
- For his breath on every stage of your preparation and delivery.

Get Specific

Ask God for specific lines, examples and illustrations that will grab people's attention and bring a point to life. When I've done this, the feedback I've received from individuals afterwards is that it was one of those illustrations that jumped out at them and that's when God started to speak specifically, when it stopped being just a nice talk and became a talk *for them*. I also often pray about what my opening sentence should be, especially if I'm speaking somewhere I've not been before.

Pray for Yourself

+ Don't just pray over your talk, pray for yourself. Pray that your own life would more and more come into line with the Bible; that your life would be God's message as well as your words.
+ Pray when you get stuck. When your preparation seems to hit a wall and you dry up – which will happen at some point in nearly every talk you write – stop and pray. Step back from your material, offer it again to God and wait on him. Then go back to the heart of your message, the main thing you really want to communicate. Sometimes it will be that you've got too immersed in the wrong detail, and taking a moment to pray, will release a new energy and focus.
+ Pray if you're nervous, and need peace and boldness.
+ Just before you speak, offer yourself to God again in prayer. Consciously remind yourself that you are just there to serve him and his people.

Pray for the Hearers

* Pray for those who are going to be listening to you
* Pray that their hearts would be open to God and what he wants to say to them.

Look to God

* Tell him what you would love to see happen in your talk and be open to him dropping in a little something, even at the last minute.
* Pray that God would be honoured by what you say, and that as he is lifted up all would be drawn to him (and not to you).
* Having put in the hard work, ask God to do whatever he wants to do, to use you however he wants to use you, to speak to you by his Holy Spirit even as you speak, to override your imperfections so that the audience might grow in their love of God and service to him.
* After you've spoken, through prayer give all praise and responsibility back to God.
* Throughout the whole process, tell God you need him. Confess your weaknesses and look to rely on him. The good news is that God's 'power shows up best in weak people' (2 Cor. 12:9, TLB).

Pause:

Spend some time asking God to help you in your journey as a speaker, that he would give you fresh insights from his Word for his people and those who don't yet know him.

18.

Phew! – After You've Spoken

After all the prep and prayer, study and sweat, a time will come when the talk will be over. When you get to the finishing line, there is no norm for how you might feel and what you should do, but here are some thoughts and ideas:

* Rest. Public speaking can be draining physically, emotionally, mentally and spiritually. So you may well feel very tired directly after speaking. Be aware of this and get some rest.
* You might find that you feel quite vulnerable. Find a safe person to be near you and pray for you immediately after you've finished.
* Some people feel completely rubbish just after they've spoken, caused by a combination of the adrenaline from the pre-talk nerves leaving the body and creating a sort of slump, and also perhaps spiritual attack. If this happens to you, try to be rational and get some rest.
* Don't pick your talk apart immediately after you've finished. Instead choose to shelve it for a day or two then come back to it critically.
* Listen to your own talks. It's not nice to begin with, but to be fair, it's no less than what you're subjecting others to,

and you will get used to it. We can only fix the things we become aware of.

- As you reflect on your talk, ask yourself some questions:

  - *If you are pleased with your talk, why was it better than others you've given?*
  - *Where did you connect well and why?*
  - *Where did you seem to lose people and why?*
  - *If you weren't happy with a talk, why?*
  - *Is there anything you wish you hadn't shared or anything you said too harshly?*
  - *How can you learn from that?*

- In advance, ask other people for honest feedback, but not just from nice people who always say nice things. I've found that for me, I am most responsive to constructive feedback a couple of days after I've spoken, because by then I am less tired and vulnerable, and more able to take their input on board.

- Decide to take criticism well (it's never easy, but it is very necessary) and to be gracious to those who give their opinion when you didn't ask for it.

- Ask God what he thought. It's easy to overlook this, but when I first started speaking and was travelling a lot, I often had no friends in the audience, so I could only look to God to be my critic. I was always amazed at the specific feedback he gave me – suddenly a part where I'd said too much, or a point that was well-made would come to mind. Now I often forget to ask him, because I speak regularly in front of friends and trusted colleagues, and have so many people willing to pass on their opinions. But of course, God's opinion matters above all others. If we ask him, he will speak to us and hone our gift.

- Review your notes and type up any changes or additions you made, either just beforehand or during your talk. Think

about those moments when the Holy Spirit dropped something in unexpectedly and add this in to your notes, so you
can include it if you use the same material again. This will
help sharpen and improve the talk each time you do it.
* Consciously choose to give any glory to God, and leave the
ultimate responsibility with him.

Pause:

*How do you feel after you've finished giving a talk? Tired
or invigorated? Up for a party or ready for some alone
time? Hugely vulnerable or on top of the world? Be
aware of your post-speaking reaction and emotions so
that you can process and rest in the way that you need
to.*

Interview

Jo Saxton

I've asked Jo to share her thoughts because she is a speaker I just love to listen to. She always holds my attention, blending raw and funny stories with hard-hitting truth. Her wisdom and passion for the Word is inspiring and infectious. I always leave one of Jo's talks with much to chew on and bring before God.

Why do we preach? What do you understand the purpose of preaching to be?

We preach to communicate and hold out the truth about God — to communicate who he is and what he's done. I think it holds up a mirror to show us the reality of who we are or where we are with God, but it should also be a map, practically showing us the way back if needed.

Have you always wanted to speak? When did you know it was part of your calling?

I remember sensing a particular call to preach at a Spring Harvest event when I was 16. I was not impressed, and was pretty terrified at the prospect. In general, I wanted the world to swallow me so I wasn't seen, so the idea of preaching was horrendous. But simultaneously, and contradictorily, I felt compelled by it.

Knowing that it was something I would do in life grew over many years. By my mid twenties, I felt sure it was an integral part of my calling, but even now (mid thirties), I don't presume it. It's something I kind of give up in my heart from time to time – it helps me keep perspective.

Can you remember the first talk you ever gave? If so, how did it go?

I do! I was 12 years old; it was a Sunday school anniversary at my church. All the youth group were involved and I was given the talk to do. It was on the gifts of the Holy Spirit, which was my choice. I remember the church pianist slamming the piano shut and walking out, I remember opening up my Bible and talking, I remember the smiles and the collective passion of the youth group. We had encountered the Holy Spirit quite powerfully, but the church at large was rather traditional. I think it went OK.

Is there any part of talk preparation or delivery that you've particularly had to work on?

Confidence was a huge issue. When I started, I was so nervous I'd be ill before and afterwards. It meant my voice would shake, I would talk really quickly, and try to avoid eye contact – not ideal. But doing theatre studies A-level helped a lot with technique and confidence. I still have to watch how fast I speak, but now it's down to excitement, rather than nerves. It's worth listening to a recording or watching a video of yourself occasionally to see what you are like. I hate doing that; I cringe and will probably always be my harshest critic, but it helps me see what I am like and how to improve.

Who has inspired you as a speaker in the past, and who do you like to listen to now?

I've always been inspired by good communicators in general. I watched a lot of Oprah! I watched how an audience were engaged, moved by the power of a story, and compelled to respond. I used to watch Ant and Dec, because they are hilarious and comic, but clean and fun. This might sound odd, as Oprah and Ant and Dec aren't preachers, but growing up I didn't see many preachers around. Later, when I was at St Tom's in Sheffield, there was a great team of preachers to learn from and be inspired by. Now, I love listening to Mike Breen, Mike Pilavachi, John Ortberg, Beth Redman, Pete Grieg, Christine Caine. I love listening to missionaries. I still watch and learn from what I see on TV – stand-up comics, talk show hosts, news readers. And though I know everyone says it – I think both Barack and Michelle Obama are great communicators.

How do you prepare your talks, and what is your starting point?

I start with prayer. Whether it's a sit down prayer time, or in the car or cooking, I ask, 'Lord, what am I supposed to say?' I consider the people I am talking to, how long I have, and pray until I get a sense of what to talk on. The topic and the Bible verses pretty much become clear at the same time. Then depending on how long I have, I just think about it for a while as I'm getting on with the rest of life – kids, work, whatever. I let it marinade. I like to look at the verses in different translations, see what there is to learn there. From that point on, I need dedicated time. Sometimes I'll look at commentaries; sometimes I'll explore the verses in their original languages. Then I get an outline together, and pray a bit about how the talk is supposed to end. Sometimes I pray for specific words for where people are at, and I pray about what stories to tell. Then I write it – well, often I preach at the wall, then run to the laptop and try to record what I've just said. Once I've written it out in full, I try to go through it a few times to hear it, to learn it. It's not always this straightforward – life gets in the way – but these are my personal ideal ingredients.

What would you say is the most important element of a talk?

So many things come to mind, but I reckon that it's very important that we are biblical.

What would you say makes a good talk, good and a bad talk, bad?

I think this is probably subjective, but I love to be challenged and stretched, and to learn; I want to take something away that is life transforming. I also like to laugh.

I can't think of many bad talks that I've heard, because you can usually glean something, learn something from a talk. In theory, I guess a bad talk is when it's insulting to other people, or a personal rant, rather than something of substance. That would be uncomfortable.

Can you think of any mistakes you've made, or problems you've had to overcome?

The biggest mistake I made was the era when I forgot that my lifestyle mattered. I did my own thing in the week, and still got up there and spoke. Theologically, I was accurate, but I was all talk, I was not living the life. I couldn't live a double life forever, and eventually it caught up with me. My heart and life was a mess. Thankfully, with Jesus there's grace to start again. So I did.

Problems I've had to overcome: I think it's been a challenge to iron out the women in leadership thing, knowing on occasions that there are people listening who don't think I should be there. Sometimes that has been hard and felt personal. Now I just respect our differences and get on with what I believe I'm supposed to do.

It's been a journey, learning to lead and preach as a woman – even to work out what to wear, what illustrations to give. It's been a journey just being comfortable in my own skin, to stand in front of people and not be intimidated, or feel I shouldn't be there. It's taken a while to be OK with being myself (though I am always nervous), and it's an ongoing journey working out my priorities. I am a preacher, a leader, but I'm also a wife and a mum, and I'm called to be those things too.

Is there a particular verse or subject you love to speak on again and again?

How God loves to transform our lives. I cannot get over the fact that God is our redeemer – redeems our lives, our communities, our world. I love to explore that as often as I can.

Do you have any top tips for engaging an audience?

Be yourself. No matter who you admire – it's natural to pick up a few traits here and there – God has called you to that audience in that moment, so let him use you, and work through you.

I like to think of who my audience are, and try to choose illustrations and observations that they may connect with, translations of the Bible that are accessible to them. I think of stories from my own experience that they might relate to, which will hopefully give them the permission to open up with the Lord and their friends about where they are at too. Also, remember your audience will not all learn in the same way. You'll have people who will learn through visuals, music, the arts, stories. I think that using different resources in a talk – film clips, music, PowerPoints, parables, drama – can all be ways the Lord gets to the audience's heart with his grace and power.

I think humour helps, as does passion about what you're saying – and that can be loud and vibrant, or quiet with depth.

Finally, the best thing is to rely on God. At the end of the day, it's all about God. And even when we feel we've nothing to offer, and we don't feel we're all that, he is all we need to offer, because he meets everyone's needs.

Jo lives in sunny southern California with her pastor hus-band Chris and their two children. She is a director of 3DM, a movement that equips churches to put disciple-ship and mission at the heart of all they do. A speaker and a writer, Jo is the author of Real God, Real Life and Influential. In her spare time she grabs a coffee, heads to the beach and wonders at God's greatness and kindness.

19.

Now What? – Where Do You Go From Here?

Before we come to the end, there is just time to pass on some general thoughts that are less about you developing as a speaker and are instead some slightly 'bigger picture' issues to consider:

- Develop an appropriately critical (though not negative) mindset when listening to other speakers. What works and why? What doesn't work and why? This can be uncomfortable for us as Christians, but it is important we learn to reflect for our own growth.
- Every speaker needs to make sure they're not a people pleaser. This might sound strange, but it's something God showed me early on. If you're too fearful of what people think of you, or if you want to look good in the eyes of other people, that will skew everything from what you preach on to how you preach it. If you know that you struggle with being too aware of what others think, then ask God to deal with it, and perhaps get some prayer, as the danger of people pleasing doesn't just apply to preaching but all aspects of leadership.

- Within reason, take seriously and consider every opportunity to teach. And not just the 'big jobs' but things like cell group, Alpha and youth group too. When I first started speaking, I felt God tell me to say yes to every invite for a season. For a while God wanted to get me practising on quite an intensive scale. The only way we'll get better is to do it.

- If you're speaking somewhere other than your home church, it's a really good idea to take someone with you. Apart from anything else you can share the driving, but more importantly it is so much better than doing things alone.

- As you wait and pray for opportunities to use your gift, don't try to force doors open but wait to be asked. Revelation 3:7 says: 'What he [God] opens no one can shut, and what he shuts no one can open.' If speaking is part of the plan for your life, you don't need to force anything. God will do it. There is such security in knowing that God has placed us where he wants us and we haven't 'made it happen'.

- If speaking is something you feel called to then put the hard work in now. Work on talks even when you don't have opportunities to speak. Go back to the Pause at the end of chapter 3 and begin to work on your ideas.

- Choose to enjoy the process of talk preparation and delivery, and don't be discouraged if you find it hard from time to time. There is a lot to worry about (you want your talks to be good, you're desperate for inspiration and you want to take the truth and put it in the best way possible) and take on board, but don't take yourself too seriously.

- If you speak often, make sure you're varying your style and structure. Don't get stuck in a rut with a three-point sermon, or unpacking a verse, or looking at a character of the Bible.

- Realize that you will get better. What is now a struggle will become easier as you practise and develop.

- Get stuck into reading and studying God's Word, so that you can say, along with Paul in 1 Corinthians 11:23, 'For I received from the Lord what I also passed on to you'.
- Review how you're doing and any challenges you need to take on. Where do you need to grow?

A Final Word

And so we have come into land. I hope that reading this book has given you lots of ideas to help you develop and deliver some excellent talks. Now you've got to the end, can I encourage you not to leave it here? Ponder, pray and mull things over. As you reflect on what you've read, don't try to take on board every piece of advice given. Pick out one or two things you could be doing better and begin to work on those. Go back and re-read the chapter that most speaks to you now. Re-read the interviews. Start putting things into practise – whether it's in your bedroom or your church. Once you begin to see change in one aspect of your communication, you can move on to another and start to work on that.

My hope for you is that you will become the best communicator you can possibly be, that many eyes will be opened to God's goodness and grace, many lives will be changed into the likeness of Jesus, many hearts will be more devoted to him, and the Church more equipped to serve this world that he so loves. God is with you and he is for you, so go for it:

Now go; I will help you speak and will teach you what to say.

Exod. 4:12

Appendix 1

A Work in Progress

Why not use these next pages to help you develop a talk idea as you work through this book?

Initial ideas and thoughts

Bible passages and notes

Ideas for your main focus

Main focus (once decided)

Main content

Ideas for an introduction

Any quotes or ideas for multimedia

Structure

How to end

What is the main thing you want to leave your listeners with?

Appendix 2

O Come Let Us Adore Him, December 2002 – Transcript

You would think that speaking the Sunday before Christmas would be the easiest gig in the Christian calendar. You would be wrong. I have agonized over this talk in the weeks and weeks since I've known I would be doing it. I even tried to get out of it, but that was unsuccessful. I've known for weeks that this night would come, and about a month ago I started stressing. I snatched minutes here and there, reading through the birth stories in the Gospels, waiting for inspiration to hit me between the eyes, but as the weeks went by and Christmas got nearer and nearer, I've found it harder and harder to set time aside.

So last Sunday was going to be my day, the day I would lock myself in my bedroom and not come out until I had heard the voice of the Almighty speak and tell me what it was we needed to hear tonight. But my Christmas tree had other plans. It viciously attached itself to my left eyeball and so I spent five hours sitting in casualty.

So I reverted to plan B, which was that I would give over the whole of Tuesday night. But then *Home Front* (BBC2, 8 p.m.) happened. 9 p.m. came round so quickly and I retired to my study – also known as my bedroom – where I promptly got distracted by my remaining unwrapped Christmas presents, which for some reason suddenly seemed particularly urgent. At 11 p.m. it was time for my bed.

It's been said before, but Christmas is a crazy, busy time. There is so much going on for everyone, and even if your very own Christmas tree does not stab you in the eye, there are always plenty of other distractions. Isn't it the cliché of the season that we 'do away with the manger' and in all the madness we forget the point of Christmas? But tonight we're here – we're not shopping, wrapping, eating, drinking, partying, stressing, or sitting in Casualty.

Tonight we can give a few minutes to looking again at that so very familiar Christmas story. In particular tonight, I want us to look at the stories of the shepherds and the wise men, and see if we can learn anything from the part they played.

So first of all, let's look at the shepherds. We read about their part in the Christmas story in Luke chapter 2, and it starts in verse 8:

> And there were shepherds living out in the fields near by, keeping watch over their flocks at night.
>
> [Luke 2:8]

OK, so the scene is set. There are shepherds – we don't know how many there were. We do know that being a shepherd wasn't the equivalent of being a merchant banker in those days. It was generally considered the job you got if you couldn't do anything else. And being a night shepherd was worse – it was considered the job you got if you couldn't do anything else, but at night. So we have a bunch of people who weren't considered much in the eyes of the community, probably therefore weren't considered much in their own eyes either. It might be fair to say that they weren't the brightest buttons in the box, the sharpest knives in the drawer, meatiest sandwiches in the fridge . . . you get the picture:

> An angel of the Lord appeared to them, and the glory of the Lord shone around them, and they were terrified. But the angel said to them, 'Do not be afraid. I bring you good news of great joy that will be for all the people. Today in the town of David a Saviour has been born to you; he is Christ the Lord. This will be a sign to you: You will find a baby wrapped in cloths and lying in a manger.'
>
> [Luke 2:9–12]

So some of the first people to hear the Christmas message were lowlife scummy shepherds. My Bible commentary points out that they were certainly an unexpected bunch, and probably a despised group of people. So many of us have grown up singing, 'While shepherds washed their socks by night. . .' and yet we see that there was something deeper going on – to a group of people looked down on by everyone else, God said, 'I choose you. I want you to play a part in the greatest story that will ever be told.' There cannot be a greater compliment, or a bigger boost to one's self-esteem than God saying, 'I choose you to bring about my purposes, to share my secrets.' That moment must have changed the lives of those people forever:

> Suddenly a great company of the heavenly host appeared with the angel, praising God and saying, 'Glory to God in the highest, and on earth peace to men on whom his favour rests.' When the angels had left them and gone into heaven, the shepherds said to one another, 'Let's go to Bethlehem and see this thing that has happened, which the Lord has told us about.'
>
> [Luke 2:13–15]

I love the reaction of the shepherds here. There's something about their response that is so sweet: 'Let's go to Bethlehem and see this thing that has happened' [Luke 2:15]. It's kind of like, 'Wicked, brilliant!', and off they all go on their donkeys or scooters, and buzzed their way out of there. It's almost quite a childlike response – let's go and check it out. But the clue to their response is in the next line, 'Let's go and see this thing that has happened, which the Lord has told us about' [Luke 2:15]. They might not have been high society, or part of Mensa, but they knew that this was a message from God (probably the heavenly host thing helped them out on that one – I would imagine it would be a fairly convincing scene) and that when God speaks you act. So off they went:

> So they hurried off and found Mary and Joseph, and the baby, who was lying in the manger. When they had seen him, they spread the word concerning what had been told them about this child, and all who heard it were amazed at what the shepherds said to them.
>
> [Luke 2:16–18]

I find this bit of the story a bit frustrating because it isn't very juicy. I like a bit of 'and he said, and she said, and no he never!', but unfortunately we don't get to listen in on what they did when they saw Jesus, what was said when they met the family. But we do get to know what their response was: 'they spread the word concerning what had been told them about this child, and all who heard it were amazed at what the shepherds said to them' [Luke 2:17–18]. God gave the shepherds the privilege of spreading the first bit of good news. He gave this awesome job, this joyful task, to shepherds – the lowest of the low. He gave them something to say, something that was worth listening to. And then thirty-three years later Jesus would give the women the job of telling the disciples that he had risen from the dead. This was in an age where a women's testimony was worth nothing, and God trusted them with the most important note of all. God is neither a snob, nor is he sexist. He will use the greatest and the least to bring about his purposes, and wants all people to know the pleasure of being part of his plans.

So that was part one – the shepherds, and we'll come back to them in a few minutes, but for now it's the turn of the Magi.

We read the story of the Magi or the wise men in Matthew chapter 2:

> After Jesus was born in Bethlehem in Judea, during the time of King Herod, Magi from the east came to Jerusalem and asked, 'Where is the one who has been born king of the Jews? We saw his star in the east and have come to worship him.'
>
> [Matt. 2:1,2]

So we welcome to the evening the Magi, who were in fact not really wise men, but astrologers. My trusted commentary tells me that they 'played a prominent part in court life in many eastern states, as advisers to the kings. Their insights were derived from sophisticated astronomical observation combined with the sort of "interpretation" which present-day horoscopes provide'. I don't know about you, but I'm now picturing Mystic Meg on a camel, which isn't necessarily helping. Anyway, my commentary continues: 'By such calculations they had concluded that an important royal birth had taken place in Palestine, which called for a "state visit".'[8] Hence they arrive in the story slap bang in Jerusalem.

Note here that we don't know how many of them there were. Apparently, we have assumed there were three because that's how many gifts they brought with them. One website that I searched on said there had to be more than two because two people would have found it hard to travel with three parcels (the editor of that particular website has obviously never seen the amount of make-up I take with me when I go away).

So, 'when King Herod heard this' [Matt 2:3] . . . to refresh your memory, the news that King Herod had just heard was not that Jamie had been written out of *EastEnders*, via shocking car accident, but that the Magi had come to worship a king. One thing we know about King Herod was that he didn't handle competition very well. On that same website I found something slightly more educational on this subject: that King Herod murdered a wife, three sons, a mother-in-law, a brother-in-law and uncle to cling to power. Two things we can learn from this: number one, being related to King Herod could seriously damage your health; number two, top of the list of things not to say to Herod would be, 'Where is the one who has been born king of the Jews? We saw his star in the east and have come to worship him' [Matt. 2:2]. But bless the Magi (definitely not wise men in this case), they weren't to know this. So:

> When King Herod heard this he was disturbed, and all Jerusalem with him. When he had called together all the people's chief priests and teachers of the law, he asked them where the Christ was to be born. 'In Bethlehem in Judea,' they replied, 'for this is what the prophet has written:
>
> '"But you, Bethlehem, in the land of Judah, are by no means least among the rulers of Judah; for out of you will come a ruler who will be the shepherd of my people Israel."'
>
> Then Herod called the Magi secretly and found out from them the exact time the star had appeared. He sent them to Bethlehem and said, 'Go and make a careful search for the child. As soon as you find him, report to me, so that I too may go and worship him.'
>
> [Matt 2:3–8]

Had pantomime been invented back then, the rest of the court would have at this point shouted out, 'Oh no he doesn't' and

King Twanky would have responded with, 'Oh yes I do', 'Oh, no he doesn't'. But thank heavens, there was not pantomime in those days:

> After they had heard the king, they went on their way, and the star they had seen in the east went ahead of them until it stopped over the place where the child was. When they saw the star, they were overjoyed. On coming to the house, they saw the child with his mother Mary, and they bowed down and worshipped him.
>
> [Matt. 2:9–11]

The Magi had come looking for a king, but didn't seem to be put off by the lack of a palace, wealth or grand surroundings. They allowed their expectations to be overridden, or maybe they just didn't have any expectations at all. Maybe they were just being obedient, following through on something they were called to do. They weren't guided by the earthly, but the heavenly. They had a mission and they chose to accept it. They had come to worship and were obedient in stopping where they were lead to stop, and they worshipped: 'Then they opened their treasures and presented him with gifts of gold and of incense and of myrrh' [Matt. 2:11].

The Magi came with their gifts. These gifts were hugely expensive, costly gifts, certainly fit for a king. In the hindsight we have in looking back over Jesus' life, we see so clearly their significance – gold, for a king, incense, for worship, and myrrh, for burial. Prophetic gifts about Jesus' life and death and who he was.

'And having been warned in a dream not to go back to Herod, they returned to their country by another route' [Matt. 2:12]. The Magi, as we see here, and generally in their part of the Christmas story, had a genuine revelation even though they weren't Jews, and weren't necessarily followers of God.

Throughout, theirs seems to have been a simple mission – one of obedience, but more of that in a minute.

So that was the Magi's part to play in the Christmas story, and in the few minutes we have left I want to just look at a couple of comparisons between the worship of the Magi and the worship of the shepherds, and how we can apply that to our own lives.

The first is that shepherds were led to worship out of their delight, and the Magi were led to worship out of their duty.

When the shepherds heard what the angels told them, they acted with eagerness. They were excited about what they'd heard and seen, and they responded.

The Magi, on the other hand, were lead by their duty. They saw in the stars that a royal birth had taken place and they responded as they were supposed to. Their journey was planned and strategic. It would have taken thought and consideration, and it cost them – to leave their homes, to live on the road for however many weeks or months, the expense of their gifts.

Another way of putting it is that the shepherds were led by their emotions and the Magi were led by their minds. Both are healthy approaches to worship. Some of us have tendencies to be more analytical and led with our mind, others of us are more emotional and tend to be led by our hearts – both are acceptable and pleasing to God, when the end result is worship. Both the Magi and the shepherds responded to revelation, and were led as a result to that place of worship, to the very place where Jesus was. According to our different characters and emotional make-up, as well as the changing circumstances of our lives, we will adore God in different ways. This is OK, as long as the result is that we do adore him. I once heard someone say that if you teach the mind and inspire the heart, you will strengthen the will. We need to feed our mind, study the Bible and learn more of who he is. We need to let our hearts be inspired with his love, with the awe of who he is. And this will lead us to worship him.

The second comparison is that the Magi brought gifts as their worship and the shepherds came simply as they were.

As part of their worship, the Magi brought gifts – costly gifts. Our worship often includes sacrifice – not sacrifices of animals or birds as we see in the Old Testament, but a conscious releasing to God of ambitions, dreams, and habits, maybe sacrifices of possessions or money, letting go of things in our life that we place a higher priority on than God. Our ultimate act of worship is handing over the whole of our lives to God and asking him to take control, knowing that because he is a good God, a loving Father, we can trust him. Worship is about surrender.

On the other hand, the Bible leaves us with no reason to believe that the shepherds brought anything with them. They didn't know they were going to meet the Son of God when they set off for work that evening. They were totally unprepared, and unless they nipped home to grab some talc from one of their mums' present drawer (don't all mums have a present drawer, ready for unexpected parties, etc.?), it's more likely they came empty-handed.

In our worship, and again at different stages of our lives, there is place for both – for coming with things to lay before him and for coming empty-handed, just as we are.

It was something I had to learn when I was going through a tough time last year – that it was OK just to be in the presence of God and not talk, pray, study, sing, think. All I could do, and all he wanted me to do, was just to be with him – an offering of my very self. I loved God – that didn't change – and so my simple act of worship was my quietness, my tears and my brokenness – and at the heart of it all a whisper in me that said, 'I love you God, I need you.'

Whether we come like the Magi – with something to offer, or more like the shepherds – empty-handed, the important thing is that we do come, we do draw near to worship, we do come to adore him.

Thirdly, the shepherds came to worship a saviour, the Magi came to worship a king.

When the angel appeared to the shepherds it said, 'Today in the town of David a Saviour has been born to you' [Luke 2:11] and they responded by going to him. The Magi, on the other hand, came for a king. The stars pointed to a royal birth, so they made their journey to worship.

In Jesus, both were satisfied. It's the same Jesus we worship – Jesus who came to live a life without sin, to die a death he didn't deserve, and to rise from the dead in order to win the battle over sin and death – to do all of this to take the punishment on our behalf and so bring us into a real relationship with a perfect God. The same Jesus, who then returned to heaven, is now seated at the right hand of God and is the King of kings, the Lord of lords, the one who is ultimately in charge, despite how things might seem sometimes from our earthly perspective.

Jesus is both King and Saviour – this is the 'Wow!' and 'Whoa!' of God.

I had the privilege recently of going snorkelling in the Barrier Reef. It was a wonderful experience. On the one hand it was so beautiful – the fish and the coral were such amazing colours. On the other hand, it was also quite scary: as I swam to the edge of the reef all I could see was pitch black nothingness. There was stunning beauty (wow!) and awesome scariness (whoa!). In the same way, God is both wow and whoa. He is good and kind, but fearsome too. Not one or the other, but both.

Jesus is both King and Saviour – both Magi and shepherd found what they were looking for. We need to remember that we don't worship just a Saviour – the one who saves in all ways. We also worship a King and he, and only he, can be in charge of our lives.

The fourth comparison is that in both cases their acts of worship were followed with a response.

When the shepherds left Jesus, their response was to tell others what they'd seen and heard. They couldn't keep it to themselves.

After the Magi had been to worship, their response was one of obedience. We read in Matthew that they didn't go back via Herod, as he had asked them to, because they were warned in a dream. They changed their plans because God intervened.

Our worship of God must make a difference in our lives. If we love him there is a response – our lives will look different as a result. We will tell others, we will follow him, we will obey him. We can't say we love him and then not do his will. In John 14:15, Jesus says, 'If you love me, you will obey what I command.' To obey is to worship. God calls us to this.

So those were just some thoughts from looking at the Magi and the shepherds. And I think the main thing I would want to leave us with, more than how they worshipped, more than what their worship looked like, is the fact that they both, in different ways, took the time to seek out Jesus and spend time adoring him. Whether we are more like the Magi or more like the shepherds, as we think about the Christmas story again, I would love our response to be a simple one of worship. Come, let us adore him. Let us put aside everything else, and worship him again tonight, our Saviour, Jesus.

Notes

[1] William Shakespeare, 'Twelfth Night', in *William Shakespeare: The Complete Works* (ed. Stanley Wells and Gary Taylor; Oxford: Oxford University Press, 1998).

[2] I am using the word 'audience' in this book to describe the group of people listening to a talk. This is because it is all-encompassing for different settings, rather than specific words such as 'congregation'.

[3] Charles Spurgeon was a famous preacher in the 1800s. In his lifetime he spoke to millions, and is still referred to by many as 'The Prince of Preachers'.

[4] John Stott, *The Contemporary Christian* (Nottingham: IVP, 1992).

[5] Howard Thurman, http://www.inspirationpeak.com (accessed 7 July 2011). Quote used with permission from publishers Beacon Press and Friends United Press.

[6] Opinions vary as to how much of our communication is non-verbal. It is thought to be somewhere between 60 and 90 per cent.

[7] Paraphrased from C.S. Lewis, *Letters to Children* (New York: MacMillan, 1985).

[8] http://oamweb.com/religious/oznan/ (accessed December 2002).

Bibliography

Every effort has been made to attain the correct copyright permission for all quoted and referenced material.

Books

Lewis, C.S. *Letters to Children* (New York: MacMillan, 1985).

Pawson, J. David. *Unlocking the Bible* (London: Collins, 2003).

Shakespeare, William. 'Twelfth Night', in *William Shakespeare: The Complete Works* (ed. Stanley Wells and Gary Taylor; Oxford: Oxford University Press, 1998).

Sorkin, Aaron. *The West Wing Script Book* (London: Channel 4, 2003).

Stanley, Andy and Lane Jones. *Communicating for a Change* (Colorado Springs, CO: Multnomah Press, 2006).

Stott, John. *The Contemporary Christian* (Nottingham: IVP, 1992).

Talks

Wilson, Ness. *Public Speaking, Preaching and Communication Skills* (a seminar at Soul Survivor 2006).

Online

http://www.inspirationpeak.com (accessed 7 July 2011).

Mukoro, Jay. 'The Art of Oratory', *BBC News Magazine* (3 April 2009) http://news.bbc.co.uk/1/hi/magazine/7981471.stm (accessed 7 July 2011).

http://oamweb.com/religious/oznan/ (accessed December 2002).

http://www.totalcommunicator.com (accessed March 2011).

Good to Grow

Building a Missional Church in the 21st Century – One Church's Story

Steve Tibbert
with Val Taylor

How does a church grow? • What are the principles involved? How do you face the challenges that growth brings?

This easy-to-read and witty account from Steve Tibbert, the senior pastor of a large and growing church in south-east London, offers principles and the odd cautionary tale to assist leaders in taking their church on a successful journey of growth, maturity and fruitfulness, maybe avoiding some painful pitfalls on the way.

In a fifteen-year transition King's Church has gone from a group of around 200 to its current position where it gathers in excess of 1,200 each Sunday. A growing church will experience growing challenges – leadership strategies and decisions can make or break the healthy development of church life. Good to Grow covers the challenges faced, both personal and corporate. The story of King's Church and God's dealings with its leaders and people will inspire and encourage you.

978-1-86024-812-2

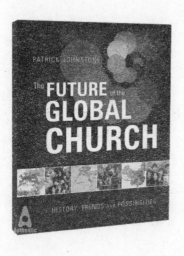

The Future of the Global Church

History, Trends and Possibilities

Patrick Johnstone

In *The Future of the Global Church*, Patrick Johnstone, author of six editions of the phenomenal prayer guide, *Operation World*, draws on his fifty years' experience to challenge us with his bold vision of the global Christian church.

The Future of the Global Church weaves together the strands of history, demographics and religion to present a breath-taking, full-colour graphical and textual overview of the past, present and possible future of the Church around the world.

978-1-85078-966-6

Growing Up

Biblical Youth Ministry
in the Local Church

Dave Fenton

At a time when young people are living increasingly stressful, pressurized lives, and leaving the church in droves, making disciples of the younger generation may seem a daunting task. But in *Growing Up*, Dave Fenton explores the whole area of effective youth ministry, providing inspiration and wisdom gleaned from years of experience, as well as offering helpful and realistic, practical advice.

A valuable addition to the Keswick Foundations series, and a 'must' for anyone working with young people who has a heart to see them grow as true followers of Christ.

978-1-85078-807-2

Gospel for Muslims

Learning to Read the Bible Through Eastern Eyes

Steve Bell

Steve Bell has thirty years' experience in cross-cultural communication of the gospel to Muslims but it was a single conversation which spurred him on to write this book. While acknowledging the challenging social and political issues posed by Islam, he explains how Muslims access the gospel more easily when it is identified with the person of the Lord Jesus Christ himself and his activity on the earth through the entire Bible – rather than with Christianity *per se*.

Bell espouses a 'third way' between Islam and Christianity, affirming the right of every Muslim to hear the good news about Jesus in appropriate ways; to change their allegiance from Islam to Christ if they so wish, and to follow him in culturally appropriate ways – even if it means doing so from outside institutionalized Christianity.

978-1-85078-880-5

Authentic

We trust you enjoyed reading this book from
Authentic Media. If you want to be informed of
any new titles from this author and other exciting
releases you can sign up to the Authentic
newsletter online:

www.authenticmedia.co.uk

Contact us
By Post: Authentic Media
52 Presley Way
Crownhill
Milton Keynes
MK8 0ES

E-mail: info@authenticmedia.co.uk

Follow us: